SCIL 1987

SCIL 1987

The Second Annual
SOFTWARE/COMPUTER/DATABASE
CONFERENCE AND EXPOSITION
for Librarians and Information Managers

Conference Proceedings
Nancy Melin Nelson, Chair

Meckler Publishing Corporation

ISBN 0-88736-194-3

MECKLER PUBLISHING CORPORATION, 11 Ferry Lane West, Westport, CT 06880
MECKLER PUBLISHING, 3 Henrietta Street, London WC2E 8LU, UK

Printed and bound in the United States of America

Contents

vi

x

Preface

The Executive Summaries for the Proceedings of Small Computers in Libraries '87 are arranged alphabetically according to speaker. When more than a single speaker authored a summary, a listing is made under all names listed on the paper. The table of contents lists only papers published here. The index, however, lists all conference speakers and their session topics, and notes which papers are not included here.

Also included in this year's proceedings is a full-length article based on a presentation made in the Exhibits Area every day during the noon break. The paper was authored by the presenter, Mark Wilson, Juniata College Library, and is also published in the March 1987 issue of *Small Computers in Libraries*.

Nancy Melin Nelson
Conference Chairperson
March 1987

smart com
macros –
  hedges
  jl lists

COMPARING GENERAL COMMUNICATIONS AND ONLINE SEARCH SOFTWARE

Ralph Alberico, James Madison University

Common Ground

There are a number of good search programs and a few duds on the market now. Choosing one isn't easy. It takes time to get to know a complex program well enough to decide if its worthwhile and reviews can't always be trusted. Another option for the searcher who wants to use the micro as a search medium is a good, general purpose communications program. Each type of program has its advantages and the searcher's choice must be guided by a variety of considerations. In each category are duds that just don't do most of the things a searcher needs done. Once they have been eliminated, the final decision is likely to hinge on the searching environment in which they'll be used and the depth of the searcher's pocketbook.

There are many things that any good communications program or search program worth its salt should do. If either type of program fails to perform all or most of these functions then it hasn't made the first cut. Here are some things to look for:

- automatic logon
- password protection
- macro creation
- uploading search statements
- simple editing for macro and file creation
- uploading files while recognizing a host prompt
- downloading to a buffer
- downloading to disk files
- scrolling backward through a search in progress
- ability to control printing while online

Extras

Beyond basic minimum requirements are those capabilities which, while nice, are not essential. Most good search programs because they were designed with the searcher in mind, provide little extras which make the searcher's job easier. Search software because, it is a specialized item, and not a mass market commodity like communications software, tends to be

1

expensive. But the high price can be justified in many search environments. Good search software is convenient. Tools for searchers are built-in; the ability to manipulate search results is often provided. Among the nice extras good search programs have are:

- a query building mode
- help and tutorials related to searching
- translation of queries
- features pre-configured for "supermarket" vendors
- features preconfigured for specific files
- ability to re-format records from online sources
- database management capabilities
- offline searching of local files
- accounting functions

High-end Communications Programs

Feature-laden, programmable communications programs offer intriguing possibilities to those willing to spend the effort required to learn to use them. Emphasis is on communications, not on post-search processing; almost total control of the communications process is possible. Scripts can be used to guide novice users and make decisions based on events in the search. Creating a turnkey system is a real possibility, but not the kind of project one embarks upon between reference questions. Among the capabilities provided by high-end communications programs are:

- scripts
- a learn mode
- programmability
- control of screen displays
- windows
- simultaneous multiple communications sessions
- user defined prompts and messages

Costs Compared

Software tools for searchers fit into four prices categories:

2

searchworks - bad online, good post-search

- low-end communications programs
    freeware to $150
    PC-TALK, <u>SMARTCOM</u>, <u>CROSSTALK</u> etc.

- low-end search programs
    $35 to $150
    ✗ DIALOGLINK, SEARCHMASTER,
    <u>SEARCHWORKS</u>, GRATEFUL MED

- high-end communications programs
    $150 to $300
    MICROSOFT ACCESS, CROSSTALK MARK IV

- high-end search programs
    $300 plus
    SCI-MATE, PRO-SEARCH [?], WILSEARCH

Tools for the Search Environment

Beyond financial considerations are factors relating to the search environment in which a program will be used. The light searcher, with a low budget, and a no frills PC might choose one of the cheaper search programs. An adaptable low-cost communications program might provide a little more flexibility, but a little less convenience. In an intensive search environment where downloading, reformatting, or local databases are emphasized, a family of expensive search tools can be worth the price. For the so-called power user, especially the individual entrusted with novice searchers and possessing the time and ability to develop local systems, a high-end programmable communications package could be the answer.

Yet another alternative is the search program which was designed for end-users, and/or for use with a specific database. The searcher who focuses on one or two databases would do well to consider a specialized program like MICRODISCLOSURE, WILSEARCH, or GRATEFUL MED. Such programs are often provided at very low cost, or as part of a subcription deal. The thing being sold is not the program, but the database its use will encourage.

3

Hardware as a Factor

The hardware used for searching is an important part of the search environment. Sophisticated high-end programs perform best on more powerful machines. Large amounts of RAM and hard disks are all but essential for the high-end search and communications programs. Don't buy a $600 program that you can't use effectively without adding a thousand dollars worth of hardware.

Choosing isn't easy. Options are increasing. Look at what you do, how you do it, and how much of it you do. Consider your financial situation. Figure out how much time and effort you want to spend tinkering with a program. Evaluate your own abilities, and those of your clients. If you go for too much you may be wasting money and time; if you don't get enough, you'll end up frustrating yourself.

Look at the information raw material you're dealing with. You don't need extensive tutorials, if you only use one or two databases and you're an expert searcher. If you run a high volume operation you might opt to forego the processing time required for a program which permits re-formatting results and go for a simpler approach. The infrequent searcher, who is apt to use numerous files and/or services, would want a lot of "friendliness" in a search program. The free-lancer would want a program capable of turning out a polished finished product. The personal researcher might want something able to handle database management tasks.

Some searchers might even want to use a few different software tools for different jobs. It's not hard to picture a search environment in which one program is used by clients, another is devoted to "quick and dirty" searching, and another to generating value-added print and online products. Nor is it hard to imagine, in the not too distant future, programs which can be adapted to different search environments, accomodating just about everyone.

4

CLONES: CAVEATS AND KUDOS

Brian Alley, Sangamon State University Library

The popular IBM PC with its open architecture design
combined with its tremendous popularity is widely recognized
as the microcomputer of choice for business and industry
as well as higher education and a host of other fields.
As the IBM PC grew in popularity it attracted a large
number of so-called aftermarket suppliers offering an
assortment of IBM PC components including everything
from memory boards to disk drives. These add-on, plug-in
components and accessories greatly enhanced the basic
PC allowing the owners to increase productivity by building
their micros into more powerful computing devices.

The popular IBM PC also inspired a number of other
manufacturers to concentrate their talents on developing
microcomputers that were compatible with the IBM design
and which could use the same software. These machines
emulated the IBM and offered products in the same general
price range. Compaq, Zenith, TeleVideo and Tandy are
a few of the popular producers of IBM compatible machines.
The compatible manufacturers have large investments in
plant and equipment and offer strong technical support.
100% compatibility with the IBM standard while offering
their own design enhancements is the goal of the compatible
manufacturers. Some, like Compaq, have prospered while
others like TeleVideo have experienced considerable difficulty
mantaining a modest market share. Yet others like Columbia
have disappeared from the marketplace altogether.

Enter the clone. If a designer can create a machine
that will run software developed for the IBM PC standard,
why not design a machine that will, for all intents and
purposes, duplicate the IBM PC in every respect? With
all those vast aftermarket and add-on parts piling up
in warehouses from San Diego to Singapore to Hong Kong
somebody had to be inspired to build the first IBM PC
clone. It was a "natural" in every respect and has resulted
in cut-throat competition that has slashed the price
of microcomputing at the IBM PC standard to well under
$1,000. per unit.

This presentation will describe the clone, its impact
on the industry and the tremendous potential it offers
for those libraries willing to assume a minor amount
of risk in order to achieve major savings in the cost
of computing. We will cover selection, purchasing, maintenance, staff training and suggestions for ways to build
a stable of clones that will do the job at less than

5

half the price of the brand name machines. At the same
time we will examine the numerous pitfalls that await
the unwary clone buyer and offer strategies for successful
clone management.

NEW TECHNOLOGY AT THE NATIONAL AGRICULTURAL LIBRARY

Pamela Q. J. Andre, National Agricultural Library

Optical technology is making important inroads into the world of libraries and information processing. The National Agricultural Library (NAL) has recognized the potential of this technology and has underway a number of projects to define and test its various uses.

NAL began its initial involvement with laser technology in the spring of 1984 with a project to master a full text file onto a laser videodisc. The USDA publication, The Pork Industry Handbook, was the first text file. This is a publication in 104 looseleaf chapters, with approximately 2 million characters of text and over 500 graphics. The disc was used with an IBM PC/XT and retrieval was provided by BRS/Search under the PCIX operating system. The system was developed by LaserData, Inc., of Lowell, Massachusetts. It was installed at 3 sites and tested for a period of 10 months. The response to this system was excellent. It was so good that a decision was made to move into Phase II, and the development of a second disc.

With the second disc, both the materials covered and the participants were expanded. Twelve U.S. government publications were selected, including The Fact Book of Agriculture, the Extension Goat Handbook, and Soil Taxonomy. The Land Grant University Libraries were invited to participate and, at this time, fifteen institutions have agreed to buy the necessary equipment to participate in the project. Work is presently underway to prepare the twelve databases for mastering. The current schedule calls for the second videodisc to be available by spring 1987.

The second new technology project involves CD-ROM technology. NAL is working with both Disclosure, Inc., of Bethesda, Maryland, and SilverPlatter, Inc., of Wellesley Hills, Massachusetts, as they prepare to put AGRICOLA on CD-ROM. AGRICOLA is the bibliographic database maintained by NAL. The expectation for this technology is wide dissemination and relatively inexpensive searching. These products are both expected in Spring 1987.

The National Agricultural Text Digitizing Project is the third new technology activity at NAL. Working cooperatively with the land grant library community, NAL is initiating a two-year pilot project to test the feasibility, cost, and effectiveness of various technologies for capturing page images, digitizing their contents, providing full text indexing and disseminating the data via optical discs. The material handled initially will be State Extension Service and State Experiment Station publications. Given a successful test, plans for the second year include the in-depth treatment of materials on Acid Rain. Primary activities at this time involve project planning and the development of grant proposals to fund the project.

Does optical technology provide a viable method of information dissemination and access? Based on its own experience, NAL votes "yes".

The Pivotal Role of the Library in Computer Integration

Wayne D. Andrews
and   Illinois State University
Alan R. Nourie

Illinois State University is a comprehensive University of approximately 20,000 students. In addition to a large IBM mainframe computing environment, the University has well in excess of 1,000 microcomputers on campus. The vision for computer literacy at Illinois State University has evolved during the past decade and has been articulated in an Academic Computer Plan. Essentially the goal is to create a computer-intensive University in which the computer will be integrated throughout the curriculum as an instructional tool where appropriate. The accomplishment of the goal will require: (a) an in-depth education and training program for faculty and staff; (b) involvement of faculty in computer-aided instruction; (c) acquisition of appropriate software tools, and (d) additional technical support personnel. In 1983, the University defined the computer literacy goal for all faculty, staff and students to acquire "basic skills". Basic skill was defined more fully but for students it meant to be acquainted with the computer as a productivity tool and to be able to use the common software related to their discipline.

The University further strengthened its commitment to computer literacy with the inclusion of a computer literacy planning statement in the 1985-1990 and 1986-91 Academic Plans. This statement was to, "establish a level of computer literacy to be achieved by faculty, staff, and students, and outline a program by which the objectives can be accomplished." A coordinator of Academic Computer Planning was appointed by the Provost for a two year term to assist in the development of planning activities. An individual was appointed by each college dean to serve as the liaison with the Provost's Office in the development of a computer plan. The outcome of these efforts was a University Plan for Academic Computing which reflected the needs and priorities of each of the colleges.

The individual college computer plans were merged at the Provost Office by the Coordinator of Academic Computing. In this process, the major priorities for each area were established and funds were allocated accordingly. It is anticipated that the colleges will re-examine their priorities from year to year as the plans are updated.

A major priority that emerged during the computer planning was a desire on the part of the English faculty to move toward the use of the computer as a tool in the English writing courses. Two years of experimental work in selected English writing sections revealed that the computer greatly enhanced the revision process in writing. Writing is taught at Illinois State University through the process approach.

In effect, students come to class each day and actually write. Students work in small groups and critique each others work. The faculty member is a facilitator. As a result of the success of their experiments, the faculty in English overwhelmingly voted to move toward using the computer as an instructional tool.

The Provost's Office, the Computer Services Director and the English Department personnel made a commitment to the project. Up front funding was to be provided by Computer Services and a small grant from the State. Students would actually support the project via a course fee of $30.00 for those enrolled in English writing. A high priority was assigned to the rehabilitation of seven class-rooms to convert them into computer instructional facilities. In addition, it was obvious from the start that other large, open access microcomputer facilities would be needed to support the number of students using the computer. Approximately 2,600 students per semester would need access to computers for English alone. As a result of these revelations, the Coordinator of Academic Computing contacted the University Librarian to discuss the possibility of providing space for a large microcomputer laboratory in Milner Library.

Conceptually, placing microcomputers in Milner seemed to make good sense. The computer is an information tool and the library is in the information business. The library has the greatest access of any building on campus. The potential for cataloging and controlling software was available. So, it was with some of these considerations that the discussions began with the University Librarian and his staff.

The Library's involvement occurred at the point where its administration was approached with a proposal that a computer laboratory be established within the main building proper. After negotiations on personnel and equipment, input was solicited from the library faculty; multiple discussions occurred; other academic institutions were contacted for information, and existing library space was evaluated. Eventually appropriate space was located; the proposal was accepted; the University Architect was involved in the planning process and physical alteration was begun. Appropriate furniture was moved and wired; a service desk was designed and constructed. Twenty student assistants were identified, interviewed and hired; the Library systems librarian agreed to administer the operation; position descriptions for civil service area supervisors (1.5 FTE) were developed and approved, and they were hired. Basic software was furnished (Wordstar initially). Finally the machines, seventy Zenith personal computers and five Apple IIe personal computers, were moved in and checked, and the seventy-five citizen printers were installed. The facility was opened for use early in the fall semester of 1986, some nine months after the initial discussions were begun.

10

HIGH SCHOOL PROGRAMS FOR ONLINE DATA

Elizabeth S. Aversa, The Catholic University of America

A survey of school library media personnel whose
programs for online data access had been identified in
early 1986 was conducted and the results of that survey
are reported here. Forty-five useable responses were
received (a 60% return rate). Findings as to levels of
students searching, databases accessed, systems used,
hardware utilized, and responsibility for the search programs were predictable: programs were primarily in the
middle and senior high schools; databases used included
news sources, current magazine indexes, and a few scientific
and technical ones; the largests vendors accounted for the
bulk of the searching; and Apple equipment was most often
used in the school setting. School media personnel most
often provided impetus for initiating search services, although teachers also began the use of online sources in
some schools. The more interesting findings from the survey
involved policies and practices regarding the MANAGEMENT of
online programs in the schools.

It was found that relatively few school programs set
policies as to how often and how long students could search,
as to who evaluated student efforts at online searching, as
to planning and budgeting for online searching, and even as
to records to be kept for administration of the programs.

11

Aversa (2)

Recommendations in the areas of instruction, budgeting,
planning, record-keeping, and evaluation of searcher
effort are discussed.

OFF-THE-SHELF: BIBLIOFILE, OCELOT AND PUBLIC QUERY TERMINALS

Richard J. Bazillion, Algoma University College

A comprehensive computerized library system can be achieved by integrating three readily-available packages: Ocelot, BiblioFile and Multilink. Once the bibliographic database exists, libraries of up to 100,000 volumes may use microcomputer equipment to automate their cataloguing, circulation, purchasing and public-inquiry functions. Because the database is created and maintained locally, membership in a centralized bibliographic utility, such as UTLAS or OCLC, is unnecessary.

The central processing unit consists of an IBM AT, with 1.5M of main memory and 115M of random-access memory provided by two daisy-chained Emerald hard disks. There is no limit on file size with the Emerald equipment, so that the entire contents of the bibliographic database may be addressed as drive "C."

Ocelot's Catalogue module contains an editing feature which permits MARC-format records in Bibliofile to be transferred, edited and stored on the hard disk. Thus the full text of "hits" does not have to be keyed in during recon projects undertaken locally. The expense of this labor-intensive activity is thereby reduced. Barcode numbers are added to each record and corresponding labels affixed to books during processing, as they circulate, or in the course of a labelling project staffed, perhaps, by students.

Once the bibliographic database is large enough to be serviceable, title records are transferred to Ocelot's circulation system. This may be a designated drive on the central hard disk, or a separate unit may be installed at the circulation desk. Transactions are recorded by wanding barcode labels on books and borrower ID cards. The circulation module produces statistical reports at scheduled intervals or on demand.

Public access to the online catalogue is provided by six PC-Shadow terminals communicating through Multilink with the main database. Internal memory of 1.5-2M is required to run BiblioFile and Multilink simultaneously. So as to avoid "jamming" the system, database maintenance should be done when the public inquiry terminals are not in use. Alternatively, BiblioFile may be connected to another micro with sufficient RAM to handle the Ocelot programs. Edited records are saved on floppy disk, to be transferred later in batch to the main database.

We have found the Ocelot system to be fairly transparent to users, who seem to be able to initiate themselves to online inquiry with minimal assistance from the staff.

13

REQUIREMENTS, SELECTION AND IMPLEMENTATION:
HOW TO GET FROM A WISH LIST TO A WORKING SYSTEM

Jane Beaumont
Library and Information Systems Consultant

This paper describes the way we would approach automation if
we lived and worked in that perfect world that we all know does
not exist. Too often, the computer or software comes first and
you have to work with what you have, or having made a careful
selection there are no funds available to do what you want.

Previous speakers (M.Weaver and B.Campbell) have discussed
the needs analysis process and the benefits of doing a
feasibility study before buying and installing a system. Having
done a feasibility study, convinced management that a
microcomputer will provide benefits and save on repetitive tasks,
the next step is to confirm your exact requirements.

REQUIREMENTS DEFINITION

Defining requirements begins with updating the functional
analysis that has been done during the feasibility study. The
purpose of this exercise is to identify information processing
that occurs in day-to-day activities and which can be automated.
It is important to differentiate between tasks that can and
should be automated and those which might benefit from changes in
manual procedures. At this point we are interested in the tasks
that will be automated. Even if you are not choosing a fully
integrated collection control system, but just implementing
general office or database applications in the library, this is
an important step.

Depending on the complexity of the system and the investment
that is being made it may be appropriate to issue a Request for
Proposal (RFP) to potential suppliers. If you do not issue an
RFP it is still useful to have on hand a list of your
requirements against which to evaluate systems.

An RFP provides the library with a vehicle to organize
the information on which you base the decision to select and
purchase a system. The structure ensures that all vendors
respond in the same format. Providing checklists and making it
as easy as possible for vendors to respond ensures there is
common basis for comparison. The RFP should contain a statement
of intent, and background information on the library, including
current computer applications and collection size. Vendors are
asked to provide information on: existing installations and
business, functions available, technical and network
capabilities, ongoing support available, hardware configuration,
costs and contractual expectations.

14

SYSTEM EVALUATION

Evaluation of the vendors' proposals involves a formal scoring of the functional portion. In order to reflect the library's priorities and mandatory requirements in the evaluation it is useful to weight (assign a % value) to the various functions after scoring. This process will usually result in a short list of preferred systems which can then be investigated further. To arrive at a final selection, hardware and costs are considered, references checked and application specific demonstrations arranged to validate the preferred vendor's proposal.

IMPLEMENTATION

Regardless of the size of the project is it essential to have someone in charge of implemetation — a champion, to use 'In Search of Excellence' terminology. Unless installation is done in an orderly manner there is very little chance of acceptance and success with the staff and users of the system. The project manager creates a task list, sets the schedule, monitors progress and supervises the library's share of implementation.

Initial implementation tasks include: site preparation, installing communications lines, development of policy parameters, installation of hardware and software, and acceptance tests. After the system is up an running there may be a period of data conversion before it can be used in a production environment. Staff must be trained, procedures adjusted and documented, and a cutover plan developed.

CONCLUSION

The process described above may seem overly complicated for the purchase of a microcomputer. However, microcomputers have brought all of us much closer to the machines and it is now our responsibility to ensure that we purchase systems that will do the job we want. Taking systematic approach such as we have described will contribute greatly to the acceptance and success of automation in a library or information centre and help to realise the full potential of microcomputer systems.

MaineCat   Fact Sheet

MAINECAT IS ...

* Greatly improved access to the wealth of materials in Maine libraries through imaginative use of new computer technology.

* An efficient, flexible and economical means by which individual libraries and groups of libraries may cooperatively prepare for further steps toward library automation and the benefits it promises to library users.

* Vastly improved access to the material in individual library collections afforded by being able to search by computer.

* A combined, statewide catalog of materials in Maine libraries stored on a high-capacity CD-ROM (or "laser") disc attached to an inexpensive personal computer, searchable by library staff or the public.

WHAT MAINECAT DOES

* Provides an efficient, low-cost and flexible way for 100 local libraries to take the first, difficult step toward bringing the benefits of automation of in-house operations to their users -- creating an electronic listing of their holdings. Observance of national standard insures compatibility with future library systems of all types.

* Opens door to eventual network connections among libraries interested in them.

* Locates for library users any one of several million volumes in over 100 Maine public, school, academic and special libraries, preparatory to requesting an item on interlibrary loan.

* Provides basis for sending user directly to nearby library owning a book, rather than making him/her wait for an interlibrary loan transaction.

* Provides to users and library staff a powerful new means of finding information in a local collection, potentially replacing the card catalog in some libraries.

* Provides a specialized catalog of the holdings of libraries in a given locality, or of a given type.

* Makes it easier to avoid duplication, develop better collections through cooperative acquisitions, each of several libraries specializing in agreed-upon subject areas.

* Transfers computer records for new titles from MaineCat directly to a local micro- or minicomputer-based circulation system in libraries that own such a system.

* Makes possible extraction of copies of a library's records from the large master MaineCat database maintained by the vendor, as needed to load into a local circulation system.

* Supports ongoing cataloging, producing not only electronic records but also catalog cards, labels and bibliographies locally as required. Allows substantial improvement in useability of catalog and reduction in staff time required for cataloging.

* Provides dial-up access to holdings and cataloging information to any library or individual with a computer and modem, by means of a CD-ROM system dedicated full-time to handling such inquiries.

* Serves as basis of possible future electronic mail system for handling interlibrary loan requests and associated messages.

WHAT IS IN MAINECAT?

* MaineCat is based on merging existing electronic records of Maine libraries created through OCLC, Marcive and Research Libraries Information Network (RLIN), more than 1.5 million in all.

16

* More than 200,000 records result from use of the Maine Card Service by 100 small and medium sized libraries.

* Includes full, standard records, in MARC (MAchine Readable Cataloging) format, assuring long-term usefulness of database.

* Includes for every title an indication of holding libraries and their local call numbers.

* Holdings of Area Resource Centers not already in computer-readable form are added as quickly as possible.

* A small number of significant items held by libraries not converting their entire collection, entered by Maine State Library staff.

* Additions cumulated and new CD-ROM issued semi-annually (more often if production costs decrease).

* Current acquisitions are added through MaineCat, Maine Card Service, tape transfers from OCLC, RLIN and Marcive.

PARTICIPATION

* Public, school, special and academic libraries eligible.

* Direct participation determined on competitive basis, criteria to be developed by Automation Committee.

* 50 libraries/year for the next 2 years will get CD-ROM drive and $500 grant toward purchase of a compatible computer (projected late 1987 cost $1000-1300) and optional printer ($300-400).

* Additional libraries willing to bear hardware costs may be allowed to participate, depending on the level of associated costs.

SCHEDULE

* First disc produced in late Fall, 1987 if approved by Legislature in Spring, 1987.

* Full implementation of all features of software by mid 1988.

MAINECAT SOFTWARE WILL ...

* Be easy to use, flexible, suitable for use by public and by students as well as by library staff.

* Allow searching by author, title, subject, series, International Standard Book Number, Library of Congress Card Number.

* Allow searching by truncated term (e.g. "comput" to bring up "computer", "computing", "computation", etc.).

* Allow combination searching (e.g. author is "Asimov" and subject is "mathematics" or "arithmetic").

* Allow a choice between exact or keyword (i.e. word appears somewhere in heading, though not necessarily at the beginning) searching on author, title, subject, series.

REQUIRED EQUIPMENT

* CD-ROM drive (provided at no cost to participants).

* A compatible personal computer, most likely an IBM or compatible computer, given current trends in development of software for use with CD-ROM.

FURTHER INFORMATION

Karl Beiser
Maine State Library Automation
Project Director
145 Harlow Street
Bangor, Maine 04401

947-8336
1-800-432-7860 (in Maine)

AUTOMATING A LOCAL TABLE OF CONTENTS SERVICE USING dBASE III

Lois M. Bellamy, University of Tennessee, Memphis
Joanne Guyton, Methodist Hospital School of Nursing

A journal table of contents service and journal check-in procedure were automated at the Methodist Hospital School of Nursing Library using an IBM PC/AT and the relational database manager, dBASE III. The advantage of a relational database manager is that information in one file can be linked with information in another file. The link is accomplished through a common field in both files. This means that one file can be used for more than one application. For instance, a patron file containing names, addresses, and telephone numbers can be used with a table of contents application, a book order application, a mailing label application and a telephone list application. This avoids re-entering some of the same data for different applications and saves disk storage space.

Five separate files, CHECKIN1.DBF, CHECKIN.DBF, CONTENTS.DBF, JOURNALS.DBF, and PATRONS.DBF, were designed to work with the journal check-in and table of contents service:

FIGURE 1. FILES USED FOR JOURNAL CHECK-IN AND TABLE OF CONTENTS SERVICE

```
Structure for database  : C: journals.dbf
Number of data records  :         111
Date of last update     : 10/28/85
Field Field name Type   Width   Dec
  1   JOURNAL   Character  60
  2   ARRIVAL   Character  30
  3   PATRONS   Numeric     2
  4   DROPPED   Logical     1
** Total **                94


Structure for database  : C: patrons.dbf
Number of data records  :         178
Date of last update     : 10/28/85
Field Field name Type   Width   Dec
  1   NAME      Character  30
  2   TITLE     Character  30
  3   ADDRESS   Character  30
  4   PHONE     Numeric     4
  5   CCENTER_NO Numeric   10
** Total **               105
```

```
Structure for database :  C: checkin1.dbf
Number of data records :                 0
Date of last update    :  10/23/85
Field Field name Type      Width  Dec
    1  JOURNAL   Character  60
    2  VOLUME    Numeric     6
    3  ISSUE     Numeric     6
    4  PART      Character   6
    5  MONTH     Character   7
    6  YEAR      Numeric     4
    7  DATE_REC  Date        8
    8  NODUPS    Logical     1
** Total **                99

Structure for database :  C: checkin.dbf
Number of data records :               931
Date of last update    :  10/23/85
Field Field name Type      Width  Dec
    1  JOURNAL   Character  60
    2  VOLUME    Numeric     6
    3  ISSUE     Numeric     6
    4  PART      Character   6
    5  MONTH     Character   7
    6  YEAR      Numeric     4
    7  DATE_REC  Date        8
** Total **                98

Structure for database :  C: contents.dbf
Number of data records :               157
Date of last update    :  10/28/85
Field Field name Type      Width  Dec
    1  JOURNAL   Character  60
    2  NAME      Character  30
** Total **                91
```

CHECKIN1.DBF is an entry file for journal issues and CHECKIN.DBF is the master file of journal issues. Each record contains the essential information for each journal issue received. Each record of the CONTENTS.DBF file contains a table of contents recipients name and a journal title. The JOURNALS.DBF file contains holdings information for each journal title along with the number of patrons receiving that journal's table of contents. Each record of the PATRONS.DBF file contains a name, title, address, telephone number and cost center number. The CONTENTS.DBF file can be linked to the CHECKIN1.DBF, CHECKIN.DBF or JOURNALS.DBF files by the common field, journal, and the PATRONS.DBF file by the common field, name.

One of the strong features of dBASE III is that it has a flexible programming language, which allows the database developer to automate most procedures. Programs contained in command files can be developed to display menus of choices and to perform procedures automatically. To display the main library menu shown below, a user at the Nursing

19

Library types in the command, **DO**,   followed by the command file name,
LIBRARY:

FIGURE 2.   SCREEN DISPLAY OF MAIN LIBRARY MENU

```
****************************************************
                     MAIN MENU
****************************************************

              1>   JOURNAL CHECK-IN
              2>   PROCESS ORDERS
              3>   SEARCH DATABASE FILES
              4>   PRODUCE REPORTS
              5>   MAKE MAILING LABELS
              6>   UPDATE FILES
              7>   SYSTEM MAINTENANCE
        Enter a Number or Type Q to QUIT-->
```

The main library menu presents the user with a choice of all the
library procedures which have been automated with dBASE III. To begin
the journal check-in process, the user types in the number 1.   The
command, **DO JOURNALS**, is automatically executed, and a new menu of
choices associated with the journal check-in process and the journal
table of contents service is displayed on the screen:

FIGURE 3.   SCREEN DISPLAY FOR JOURNALS CHECK-IN MENU

```
************************************************************************
                     JOURNALS CHECK-IN
************************************************************************

          1> ENTER NEW JOURNAL ISSUES
          2> SELECT NUMBER 2 IF YOU WISH TO VIEW OR EDIT THE
             JOURNAL ENTRY FILE
          3> DETERMINE WHO NEEDS TABLE OF CONTENTS
          4> UPDATE MASTER FILE OF JOURNAL ISSUES AND MAKE BACKUPS
             PLACE JOURNALS BACKUP DISKETTE IN DRIVE A
        Enter a Number or Type R to RETURN to Main Menu-->
```

When the user selects number 1 from this menu, the command file,
BEGIN.PRG, is called, the user is prompted for information concerning
the journal issue. Two essential checks have been built into the
program. The first check alerts the user to the presence or absence of
the journal title in the journal holdings file, and the second flags
any duplicate journal issues.   The first check is important if one
wishes to produce a list of journals currently received. The second
check is necessary to avoid distributing duplicate table of contents to
patrons. Once the checks are complete, the journal issue information
is added to the interim entry file, CHECKIN1.DBF. When the user is
satisfied the entries are correct, he or she may type in number 3 from
the journal check-in menu to produce a report of the people who wish
to receive the photocopied table of contents of the new journal issues:

FIGURE 4. SAMPLE TABLE OF CONTENTS REPORT

Page No.   1
10/23/86

TABLE OF CONTENTS TO BE MAILED

** Journal Title: AMERICAN JOURNAL OF NURSING, OCT
* Number of Copies: 5
MARY JANE BUSH   SON A205
SUZANNE BLEVINS   SON A210
JACKIE BROWN   SON A203
GINNY PRESGROVE   NURSING SERVICE, CENTRAL
JEAN REED   2 WEST, CENTRAL

**Journal Title: CHRONICAL OF HIGHER EDUCATION, OCT 23
* Number of Copies: 1
MARY JANE BUSH   SON A205

**Journal Title: FAMILY AND COMMUNITY HEALTH, NOV
* Number of Copies: 1
LAURE HUGHES   SON A217

**Journal Title: JOURNAL OF GERONTOLOGICAL NURSING, SEP
* Number of Copies: 3
VIRGINIA NORTON   SON A201
KATHY MADER   6 EAST, CENTRAL
PAULA MASON   8 CREWS, CENTRAL

**Journal Title: JOURNAL OF NURSE-MIDWIFERY, SEP/OCT
* Number of Copies: 2
MARY RUTH HALLUM   SON A204
JUDY COLE   SON A211

**Journal Title: NURSING AND HEALTH CARE, OCT
* Number of Copies: 1
KATHRYN SKINNER   NURSING SERVICE

Four data files are used to produce the report: CHECKIN1.DBF, CONTENTS.DBF, PATRONS.DBF, and JOURNALS.DBF. CHECKIN1.DBF provides the journal titles and issue month for which there are no duplicates. CONTENTS.DBF provides the names of the people receiving the journal table of contents. PATRONS.DBF provides the person's address and JOURNALS.DBF provides the number of copies to make for each journal's table of contents. After the report is printed, the user types in the number 4 from the journal check-in menu to update the master file and make backup copies of the data files. When all procedures have been completed, the user types in the letter R to return to the main library menu.

If mailing labels are desired, the user can load labels in the printer, type in the number 5 from the main menu, and have labels printed for all table of contents recipients. The following additional reports using the data files singly or in combination can be produced by selecting number 4: 1) table of contents recipients and a list of the journal table of contents each receives 2) journal titles currently received 3) journal claims report. Updating and searching the data files can be accomplished by making the appropriate selections from the main menu.

AN ELECTRONIC BULLETIN BOARD IN AN ACADEMIC LIBRARY

Rebecca A. Bills, West Virginia College of Graduate Studies

West Virginia College of Graduate Studies (COGS) serves a student population of over 3,000 working professionals geographically dispersed over a mountainous, rural, sixteen-county area of southern West Virginia. The philosophy of the institution is to take the education to the student at the convenience of the student. Consequently, nearly all classes are held at night or on weekends and professors travel to various sites over the area to teach them.

In providing library services, we go to the students also. Database searches are performed for those without access to printed indexes. Requests for materials based on these bibliographies are sent to users through the mail. Books or article reprints from our collection or interlibrary loan are then sent to the student at home. Soon, dial-up access to our online catalog will be available.

With such a dispersed student body, COGS is constantly looking for ways to improve communications with the students away from the immediate area. An electronic bulletin board had been discussed for several years prior to my arrival. At that time it was decided that the library would tackle the project.

The bulletin board software program, RBBS-PC (Remote Bulletin Board for Personal Computers) is a shareware program-- it can be passed along at no charge if not altered. Users are requested to register copies with the Capital PC Users Group, members of which developed the program. The software runs on an IBM PC-XT with 640K and a 10 MB hard disk drive. The bulletin board is "up" from 3 p.m. each afternoon to the following morning at 10 a.m., and 24 hrs/day on the weekend, thus complementing the class schedule and free time of our working students.

Several types of communication are supported on the bulletin board:

1. Bulletins - information fairly constant over a period of weeks, i.e., area library hours, class schedules.

2. Messages - can be public (everyone can read) or private (only accessible to the intended receiver).

3. File transfer - public domain software, class papers, joint faculty publications, etc.

4. Conferences - although not currently in operation, conferences are designed for a specific subset, such as the members of a particular class. Access to the conference is limited to pre-specified individuals.

To instruct potential callers in the use of the bulletin board, an instruction sheet (similar to a pathfinder) is distributed to students. In the Spring of 1986 a faculty - staff - student workshop was held. A class in microcomputer telecommunications includes demonstrations and practice in using the board.

The system is used regularly by students and faculty both for coursework and for recreational purposes. A number of calls are also received from non-institutional users. Although access is open and anyone is welcome to use the system for educational purposes, the phone number is not widely published, and there is not very much of interest to those not involved with COGS. In the first 18 months of operation only one "hacker" has been encountered and was easily dealt with.

Future plans for the bulletin board include more publicity internally to increase usage. Some projects under consideration are to hold another workshop, to distribute more printed literature, and to pick a specific application and work on building it up, i.e., a particular course or faculty member.

We see the bulletin board as a positive addition to the library services we provide, although we feel we are just scratching the surface. As access to computer equipment and familiarity with it increase, we expect the role of the electronic bulletin board grow as well.

PC-DOS: ENHANCEMENT THROUGH BATCH FILE DEVELOPMENT

Neil Brearley, Carleton University

It frequently happens that one PC equipped with a hard disk has to serve the needs of several users. Often, a number of applications will be installed on the machine. The conventional configuration in such cases sees each application assigned to a DOS directory, with the individual users maintaining their working files in sub-directories. However, tree-like directory structures of this nature can be intimidating to users not familiar with DOS.

Most users need know little more than how to format a disk, copy a file or start an application. Batch files give the system administrator a means of simplifying access to applications and their related work files for any number of users, and can be used to create a shell-like environment in which file structures and DOS commands are presented in an more approachable menu format. Batch is, in effect, a programming language. As well as incorporating all valid DOS commands, it can be used to pass parameters entered at the DOS prompt, and can include such constructs as IF...GOTO and FOR...DO. Batch files are regular text files with a .BAT file extension, and are directly executable from the DOS prompt. They can be created by any word-processor having a "non-document" mode, by the DOS-supplied line editor EDLIN or, for short files, by using the COPY CON: command.

The most familiar batch file is AUTOEXEC.BAT, used to execute a series of commands on system start-up. A simple application-oriented batch file in the root directory would similarly execute a series of commands which would take the user to the directory in which the work files are held, call an application program, and return to the root directory upon exit from the application. For applications that do not recognise DOS directories, batch commands can be used to copy files to a RAM drive, or to call the SUBST command to substitute a drive letter for a directory path. A variant of the simple file would enable the user to enter his or her name or other ID when invoking an application, and would change the directory to that containing the appropriate work files. Further development would present the user with a menu of choices, determined by a batch file invoked by the AUTOEXEC.BAT file.

Two disadvantages of batch file operations should be noted. Batch files cannot be nested, it is not possible to call one file from another and have control return to the first unless a secondary command processor has been installed, although repetitive operation of a single file is permitted. Secondly, once started, the program cannot pause

and accept operator input. If the batch program is used to
display a menu of choices, it should end with a special
version of the PROMPT command, with subsequent operations
controlled by further batch files.

    Batch is not a well-documented feature of DOS, but it
more than repays study.   Experimentation and careful
attention to design will enable the system manager to create
an environment far removed from that represented by the basic
DOS 'C>' prompt.

ILL STATISTICAL DATA COLLECTION BY MEANS OF SYMPHONY 1.1

Robert W. Burns, Jr., Colorado State University Libraries

This paper will discuss the preparation of a monthly Interlibrary Loan Statistical Report using the spreadsheet (SHEET) working environment of SYMPHONY 1.1

The program operates on an NCR PC 6 Model 1015 under MS-DOS with one floppy and 10 MB of hard disk (streamer tape backup) plus 640 K of RAM. Reports are printed on an OKIDATA 193 I full carriage printer.

The report itself consists of four tables, a set of operator instructions, a short description of the program, and a Table of contents to facilitate moving from Table to Table. Special attention has been given in the design of the spread sheet to minimizing operator participation at all levels especially in the number of operator keystrokes required to input data. Print Setting sheets as well as Database Setting sheets have been prepared so that the user can easily print individual tables as separate reports or print a monthly report showing all tables. The following information is available in table form: LIBRARY CODES, ITEMS BORROWED, ITEMS LOANED, and a MASTER STATISTICAL SUMMARY for the entire year.

The spreadsheet uses a variety of functions all transparent to the user: @ NOW, @ SUM, @ IF, and @ VLOOKUP plus MENU, QUERY, and RECORD-SORT to alphabetize the file. These functions enter the current date, enter the full library name for an operator entered three letter code, perform arithmetic operations on monthly data, enter year to date (YTD) summaries, run comparisons, and transfer monthly data to the annual statistical summary report.

The application works well and saves many hours of manual arithmetic and alphabetizing of ILL Loan forms.

WHY YOU NEED A CONSULTANT

Bonnie Campbell, Ontario Ministry of Citizenship and Culture

Until very recently, sophisticated library collection management systems which handle circulation control and online catalogues were available only to large libraries. However, in the last few years microcomputer-based systems have developed to handle these functions and for the first time they are available to smaller libraries. In 1985 the Government of Ontario established a funding program to assist small public libraries (those serving populations of less than 50,000) to purchase these systems.

However, criteria for funding requires that a full feasibility study and system selection process be undertaken. This is simply good practice in any situation dealing with automation, but is especially important for small public libraries. In most of these libraries there is little or no prior experience with computers, and many miconceptions about automation.

These misconceptions include the belief that microcomputers are inexpensive, that hardware is the only cost, that a computer will reduce operating costs, that a computer will last forever, and that a system can be installed quickly and easily.

The reality is that while a microcomputer for word processing or spreadsheet analysis is inexpensive, a system for circulation control can cost in the neighbourhood of $100,000. The cost to create a database can range from $50,000 to $100,000, depending on size and method chosen. There are no cost savings to be gleaned from such a system, and there is probably a cost increase in terms of the annual maintenance cost. The system will take time, very careful planning, retraining and very careful management to be installed. And it will all have to be done again within five years, because computer systems have a life span of about that duration.

Because of the high stakes involved in such a project, the librarian is well advised to hire a library automation consultant. The consultant brings experience with similar projects and expertise in library automation. This experience and expertise means that the consultant knows what questions to ask and can guide staff through the feasibility and decision-making process. In addition, the consultant provides credibility when it comes time to ask for funds from the city government.

Cooperative Cohabitation
Libraries and Computer Learning Centers

Jennifer Cargill, Texas Tech University Libraries

The unfinished West Basement of the Texas Tech University Library was designated to be an Advanced Technology Learning Center (ATLC). The ATLC and the University Library are administered separately though these two service components within the same building both report to the Vice-President for Academic Affairs and Research. Several operational issues had to be resolved in order that both organizations could function effectively.

The 25,000-square foot facility was designed to provide state-of-the-art computer and communications technology to help students learn to use microcomputers and access mainframes to more effectively and efficiently complete assignments, and to assist professors with their courses. The center was to be a resource for improving instructional quality with the aid of computers. The major portion of the facilities' construction was completed by Fall 1985 and the staff moved in. During the Spring of 1987, the final major construction phase for the facility has been underway with the completion of a computer room to house the academic computers. With the installation of these academic computers within ATLC and in the University Library building the facility will be the major resource supporting academic research and instruction though some academic use of the administrative computing facilities will continue. The major academic computer will also support the academic network being installed in 1987 which in turn will link computers in other academic buildings. The network will be installed in an existing tunnel system through which there is access to more than 200 buildings. Ultimately, the library online catalog will be accessible through this network.

The library staff has assumed the position that having the ATLC in the library building has several distinct advantages:

* it adds a new dimension to providing information and recreation on campus;

* there will be an opportunity for increased exposure to technology;

* the center is popular, and will provide access to software and hardware to a large segment of the university community; and

* the center potentially provides developmental opportunities.

29

In order to work with a consultant, the library staff
must understand their needs and what is required of the
consultant. Most important, the staff should feel
comfortable with the consultant. The feasibility study and
system selection process is a learning experience for the
library staff and their Board and any and all questions
should be answered fully. Finally, the library staff and
Board must understand that the responsibility for a
decision to automate and the choice of a system is theirs.
The consultant can discuss alternatives and make a
recommendation but the decision rests with the library.

In selecting a consultant, the library staff should ask
for competitive bids based on a request for proposal (RFP)
which describes clearly what the consultant is required to
do, the time frames involved and how the staff expect to
interact with the consultant. The proposals and an
interview will allow the staff to evaluate the experience
and expertise of the consultants and how well the
"chemistry" between them works.

Once the consultant is hired, success for the project
depends as always on good communication. The library
manager must assure that staff are fully informed about the
consultant's tasks and that the consultant has full access
to staff and other sources of information. Staff should
all feel free to ask those "dumb" questions which always
turn out to be the ones that provide critical answers. And
the consultant should be required to make formal reports at
pre-specified checkpoints.

If all goes well, at the end of the feasibility study
and system selection process the library staff and Board
will know a great deal more about automation than when they
started. They can then move on to the purchase of their
system and the implementation phase knowing what the
trade-offs were, and what the strengths and weaknesses of
their chosen system are. Surprises and problems will
arise, but should be minimized.

In addition, having the traditional library materials
and new technology in the same physical facility supports the
concept of an information center, an information hub. The
library had pursued a traditional role, then moved toward
database access, and in the future will be more involved in
management of computer aspects. Microcomputing centers such
as are being created, put the computing power into the hands
of individuals. Of course this major impact of technology
on campus also leads to increased expectations in information
access.

From opening day, the library administration and the ATLC
staff were determined that patrons could move freely between
the traditional library environment of books, serials, and
microforms and the high tech facility of microcomputers and
terminals. Passages were unlocked, similar open hours were
scheduled and a philosophy of interaction and cooperation
between the respective staff was espoused.

This paper will focus on two issues:

* the advantage of these two facilities occupying
  the same building, in effect creating an information
  center blending the old and the new;

* the implications in general for the future of libraries
  and computer centers as information clusters; and

* the considerations for effective daily operation
  of the shared facilities.

USING DBASE III TO PREPARE MATERIAL FOR COMPUTERIZED TYPESETTING

James Carroll, Kansas State Library

This paper will explore the use of dBASE III to create documents with embedded typesetting commands. In November of 1984 John Bye, Archivist for the North Dakota Institute for Regional Studies received a grant for the production of a guide to the Institute's manuscript collections. He approached Jim Carroll, then Automation Librarian for the North Dakota State University Library, to explore the possibility of using the Library's microcomputer to speed production of the guide. After some discussion, it was decided to enter the information into a dBASE III file, where it could be easily edited and formatted for printing. Further investigation revealed that a local printer could accept documents transmitted over the telephone line for printing; moreover, these documents could have typesetting commands embedded in the text. After examining the cost of having the printer manually enter the text into the typesetter and the possibility of using our own daisywheel printer print the camera-ready output, it was decided to go ahead and use dBASE III to enter the information and produce an ASCII file with embedded typesetting commands.

It was planned to enter the data into a dBASE III database, then use a command file to send the data to an ASCII file, formatting it and adding the typesetting commands in the process. The ASCII file could then be edited one last time using PC Write and transmitted to the printer. The dBASE III database was designed to follow AACR2 format as closely as possible. Fields were established for the main entry; the title of the material; the date and physical description; biographical notes; scope and contents; donor; finding aids (if any); NUCMC number; notes; and the Institute collection number. A format file for entering data was created and student workers were hired to enter the data. While the students were entering the data, command files were written that would index the database, provide for editing the data, and would produce the formatted ASCII files. At this point difficulties arose because it had been hoped that the scope and content field could be entered into a memo field for easy editing. However, we discovered that dBASE III does not allow formatted printing of memos. Eventually, we decided on using four character fields, 256 characters wide. This proved acceptable for over 95% of the entries. For the remaining 5%, the hash mark (#) was entered as the last symbol of the field. During the final edit, PC Write would search for this symbol and the remaining information entered.

After the initial problems were worked out, production proceeded smoothly. Student workers commented that using a forms-oriented approach to data entry made the process faster and simpler, since they did not have to worry about formatting the final product. The importance of keeping backups was emphasized when a magnet was accidentally placed next to some of the master diskettes. Luckily, only a few day's work was lost and the information was quickly re-created. Because we were able to create text files that were formatted like the final output, we were able to proofread the product before sending it to the printer. Proofs were received from the printer within four days after the data was transmitted, corrections were made, and camera-ready copy was ready less than a week later.

This process proved to be less expensive than the other approaches investigated. How much less is difficult to estimate, since our production schedule and processes would have been much different if we had manually entered the information into the typesetter. If we had arranged to have the printer manually enter and format the information, the typesetting would have cost at least $650, or 30% more than transmitting the information with imbedded typesetting commands. This does not include any hidden costs, i.e., the time and money spent correcting the printer's data entry errors. Our manuscript information was usually contained on hand-written notes and we would have had to manually enter and format the information using a word processor. This would have slowed down the rate of data entry and increased our student worker and proofreading costs. Counting the costs of programming time, proofreading before typesetting, typesetting, and the cost of student workers, the project cost $1570. Had we done this manually, it is safe to assume we would have spent at least $1900 on preparations, proofreading, and typesetting. The cost of using our daisywheel printer to produce the final output would have been prohibitive in terms of time spent in cut-and-paste layout (given the programs available to us at the time) and the results would not have been professional.

PENNSYLVANIA'S CD-ROM STATEWIDE UNION CATALOG

Richard E. Cassel, Pennsylvania State Library
Department of Education

The School Library Catalog Program, a component of
ACCESS PENNSYLVANIA, has provided students, teachers and
other patrons with information about, and access to, the
resources of school, university and public libraries across
the state. The program has created an automated database
of library catalogs which is accessed via computer through
CD-ROM laser technology.

CD-ROM is an amazing new technology that utilizes a
laser light beam so tiny that 15,000 tracks of information
per inch can be placed on the disc. This technology
permitted Pennsylvania to place 650,000 unique catalog
records from 153 participating libraries on a small 4 3/4"
silver disc. An inexpensive ($650) laser reader is con-
nected to a standard IBM microcomputer which can search the
disc and find a single record, within the 650,000 records,
in just a few seconds. This amazing system has provided a
quantum leap in finding and managing information. Changing
from "linear" searching (thumbing through card catalogs) to
"logic" searching allows a user to enter several key
subject words and the computer will then find all records
containing those words. This means a user no longer needs
to know the actual title and author but can allow the
computer to find items, identified only by subject, even if
they reside in other libraries across the state.

The search software permits ease of access and provides prompts for the user. It indicates how many items
have been found and allows the user to browse back and
forth to prior screens if necessary. The user can also
print out the bibiliographic citations for use in locating
materials and creating a bibiliography for a research
report. Students are finding and using materials much more
effectively than they had been through use of the traditional card catalog. Libraries are expressing dramatic
increases in the use of materials on site. One secondary
school library reported that for October 1985 their circulation was 252. After installing the compact laser disc
database, the circulation for October 1986 increased to
2,602!

It has been predicted that CD-ROM laser technology may
be as significant for finding and accessing information as
Gutenberg's technology was in producing and storing it.

The School Library Catalog Program, which includes retrospective conversion to full MARC records, will accomplish two major objectives:

1. Provide library users with access to the books, journals, media and other information needed, not only from their own library but also any participating school, public or college library in the Commonwealth.

2. Provide a way to facilitate the automation of many time consuming library management functions such as cataloging, circulation and inventory so that librarians can use their special skills to work directly with teachers, students and other patrons.

The first year of the project utilized $400,000 of federal grant money to implement the program in ten consortiums, involving the collections of 153 libraries. The project has demonstrated that school administrators are interested in resource sharing as a cost effective way to provide students with the broadest array of library materials possible. Since Pennsylvania has used a statewide contract approach, the costs of library automation have been reduced more than 30 percent and the technical quality of data necessary for electronic catalogs and library automation has been maintained.

Currently, Pennsylvania is updating the catalog and expects to press new discs by June 1987. The new catalog database will contain approximately 1.4 million unique records and will require two CD-ROM discs. Enhanced search software will make the two discs transparent to the user and provide additional search and telecommunication options.

SPREADSHEET OR DATABASE:
Making the Most of Numeric Database Software

Philip M. Clark, St. John's University

Since the introduction of Lotus 1-2-3, there have been many attempts to integrate or incorporate features found on other programs into new programs. Lotus had the foresight to recognize that spreadsheet users wanted some form of data management and graphics capability (the 2 and 3 in Lotus 1-2-3). Symphony and Framework were the logical next step in this progression and brought into one environment the spreadsheet, database manager, graphics, word processing, and communications.

Programs like Symphony and Framework have their place and their diehard adherents, of course. But they have not replaced the standalone word processor, spreadsheet, or database manager as was predicted just a few short years ago. In general, any given module has less power and flexibility than its standalone counterpart.

For people who are dealing primarily with the analysis of numeric data, the full functioned spreadsheet program has been the program of continued choice. This is not to say that database management programs such as dBase are not used for number handling. They have always been heavily used for accounting system input and reporting. The sheer volume of income and expense transactions that can take place over the course of a year could simply not be handled efficiently on early spreadsheet programs where a matrix of 64 columns by 256 rows was commonplace.

The strength of the spreadsheet program was that it could easily compute totals, subtotals, averages and the like as well as perform sophisticated mathematical computations. In effect, it was more of an analytical tool than a processor of transactional data.

Not withstanding these differences, the users of both types of software wanted the features of the other. Spreadsheet users want to easily search for records that meet specified criteria. They also want larger workspaces for larger data sets. Database users want the built in financial, statistical and mathematical functions enjoyed by spreadsheet users. Both, in my view, want easier generation and formatting of reports they prepare from their data be it a budget balance statement or a graph of monthly activity.

In the last two years, several programs have appeared on the market that attempt to bridge this gap. The most common term I've seen used for them is analytical databases. They include Reflex: The Analyst, Paradox, and Javelin, specifically. Also, the analytical capabilities of such programs as PFS: Professional File, dBase III Plus, Rbase System V, and others have been improved greatly from their earlier counterparts.

What are some of these features of analytical databases and why might you consider using one? I'll use two programs to illustrate: Reflex and Javelin. I choose these because I own them, they're much less expensive than programs such as Paradox and Rbase System V (I bought each for less than $100) and yet they provide a full range of data management and analytical routines.

Reflex touts its multiple views of your database. You can look at a single record or a list of records. You can graph the data much more simply than you can in spreadsheet programs. It has featured a Crosstab View from the start which is only now being incorporated into programs such as PFS: Professional File and Rbase System V. It's Report View has been reviewed as the best report generator for Lotus.

Calculated fields allow the user to enter all the complex formulas that are familiar to spreadsheet users. These can be used within a given record or in summary fashion in the Report View. Extensive date functions are available to calculate days, months, or years between dates. And, a searching engine is incorporated that uses boolean logic to find groups of records that meet specified criteria. Once the criteria have been set, records can be retrieved that meet the criteria and reports and analyses performed on only those records through a filtering process. In effect, subsets of the database are created.

Javelin, on the other hand, is oriented to time series data: for example, the analysis of the day by day circulation activity in a library. It too has multiple views of a central database. Its views show the relationships between dependent variables, lists by time period, the elements making up formulas, charts that can even be used for data entry, a worksheet view that resembles a spreadsheet, graphs, and more. Of special interest to those with multiple outlets, a type of organzation chart can be designed (called a building block view) showing each outlet. Data can then be consolidated easily for each level in the organization from the most detailed to the system level.

Analytical database managers give us new tools to use in the summary and analysis of our operational data. They also provide us with the opportunity to move beyond mere description of "what is" to questions of "what if".

STARTING FROM SCRATCH
IN A NEW, SPECIALIZED INFORMATION CENTER

Sharon D. Cline, EBSCO Subscription Services

"Silicon Valley" refers to a geographic area about 25
miles long and 10 miles wide, extending from San Jose,
California, northwest up the San Francisco peninsula. It is
roughly equivalent to Santa Clara County, California. Its
nickname comes from the dense concentration of high-
technology companies, many of which produce or incorporate
into computer systems, tiny integrated circuits on slivers
of silicon, called "silicon chips." The geographic location
of Silicon Valley is due primarily to the fact that most of
the companies were started by engineers who graduated from
Stanford University, located in the heart of the Valley.
The human population of Silicon Valley is also densely
concentrated and highly differentiated, with associated
social and psychological problems that intrigue the sociolo-
gist and psychologist. Change is constant and the future is
hard to predict. The phenomena of overnight millionaires is
often balanced by widespread layoffs during the "slump"
periods. Local inhabitants include venture capitalists,
"headhunters," and entrepreneurs; as well as the executives,
managers, technical professionals, and clerical and production workers involved in high-technology companies and
institutes. The atmosphere in Silicon Valley has been
compared to the Gold Rush era because of the desire to "get
rich quick," and a popular book was written by Everett
Rogers and Judith Larsen entitled Silicon Valley Fever,
which deals with many of the psychological ups and downs
indigenous to the area.

The Silicon Valley Information Center grew out of a
need identified in part by these authors during their
research for that book. They found it extremely difficult
to find information, and had to go digging for it in many
different places. They discovered that much of the information was squirreled away in file cabinets or boxes in
storage rooms in the companies themselves; and, while the
companies had no objections to letting others inspect the
files, there was no standard or convenient way of making it
available. Also, in many cases where companies had failed,
and had gone out of business or were merged with another
company, the information was lost entirely. These observations, added to the growing number of questions on Silicon
Valley companies, individuals and living conditions which
were received by the San Jose Public Library's reference
desk, led to a successful request from SJPL for a planning
grant from the California State Library to study the situation and come up with a solution. The Silicon Valley
Information Center is that solution.

The Silicon Valley Information Center (S.V.I.C.) was officially opened on September 4, 1986, in a ceremony directed by Monica Ertel of Apple Computer, Inc., and Chair of the S.V.I.C. Advisory Board. San Jose Mayor Tom McEnery highlighted the ceremony by unveiling a neon sculpture marking the entrance to the Center, which was created by a local artist and donated to the Center by the Friends of the Library.

The grand opening marked the end of nearly twelve months of development, supported by $408,000 in Federal and local funding. The majority of these monies ($338,000) came from an LSCA grant (Library Services and Construction Act), administered through the California State Library. The remaining funds ($70,000) were provided by the City of San Jose for an online catalog system to give immediate access to the catalog of the items in the collection from terminals located in the Center, and from outside through dialup modems. Support was obtained for the second year of the project, totalling $480,000 -- $340,000 from LSCA plus $140,000 from the City of San Jose. These funds will enable the Center to establish itself in the community by demonstrating the value of its collection and services. Then, future funding will come from the City and outside private organizations and foundations.

The staff of the Silicon Valley Information Center has now experienced part of the second phase of the project: providing service to the public. Since the Center is self-contained, individual staff responsibilities include a wider range of duties than most typical library jobs; and the duties take on a slightly different nature. Many times questions come in from places far away from the immediate locale. Already, kudos are coming in from users who claim they could not have found the information anywhere else, or they couldn't have found everything in one place. But the biggest challenge is yet to come: a never-ending need to constantly document history as it happens.

CATCHING UP TO ONLINE

presented by Lucinda D. Conger

Coordinator, Online Services,

State Department Library

Washington, DC

Some time ago, I wrote a column for DATABASE Magazine on keeping up with online. That column presupposed that you were already online. This session will be addressed to those of you who are about to go online or have been online only a short time. I will presume you already have the equipment and that you have mastered your telecommunications program to the extent that you can make contact with an external service: a bulletin board, an electronic mail service, the Source, whatever. You have flexed your wings a little and now you would like to fly. What do you do next?

Well, I hate to bring you down to earth, but first there is the question of money. How much do you have to spend? Do you want to pay as you go, or do you want to investigate some of the group discount opportunities available and put down some of the money up front?

How much time do you want to invest in learning a system? Does it make any difference to you whether you can understand what is going on or do you just want the push-button mode of operation? There are trade-offs, but will it make any difference?

What are the various modes of operation that are available? What are the characteristics of some of the major searching systems? Which ones are user friendly and what does that mean precisely? What search aids are available to help you construct a search both before and during an online search session?

Is there any particular index or database that you particularly want to use or have access to? If database selection is a big mystery to you, what options do you have to help you make this choice?

How do you find out what databases there are? What are some of the major directories and other publications in the field that can help you? Who can help you with your online questions and how can you use online services to get answers?

It may be that after all is said and done, you will not even want to leave the nest. Online is not the only way to fly these days. CD-ROM and laser disks offer offline alternatives to online searching wherein costs are predictable and there is no stress of working with the meter running. And these new technologies, even more than online searching, are microcomputer-dependent.

THE USE OF askSAM, A FULL-TEXT DATABASE PROGRAM, AS AN ADDED VALUE ENHANCER TO ONLINE SEARCHING

John C. Cosgriff Jr., Virginia Tech

Most database software is designed for the business user. Consequently, most databases do not work well with the long textual fields desired by librarians. Recently, however, a number of personal computer databases have appeared which are designed to handle text. One of the best of these is askSAM, a free-form, text-oriented data base management system from Seaside Software in Perry, Florida.

askSAM has the following strengths:

1. it can quickly retrieve any word or number anywhere in a file by full-record scanning, by Boolean logic, by phrase searching, or by key-word in field;

2. it can import any ASCII file including those created by OCLC, STN International, Dialog, Medline, Wilsonline, etc. without prior editing;

3. if you desire fields for sorting and other manipulation, they can be implied, contextual, or explicit; and they do not have to be fixed length or even specified ahead of time;

4. with askSAM you can edit within a record, within a file, or from one askSAM file to another;

5. askSAM keeps the file size small by eliminating spaces, yet it can be read in its raw form, or it can be exported in ASCII format to a word processor.

One of the many applications of askSAM is in online searching. I search a number of different databases from more than one utility. When I do a literature search, I always capture it on disk (downloading), and later print it out. As you know, sometimes what you capture not relevant, and often what you capture is in small answer sets from various search strategies. With askSAM it is relatively simple to select only the relevant articles from these small sets, and sort them prior to printing them.

To import a downloaded file into askSAM, I set the record length at 20 lines maximum (or one screen), and have whatever is divided by a blank line imported as a separate record. In general, this equates to one captured item per record.

The second method I sometimes use is to first edit the downloaded search with a word processor before importing it into askSAM. Since the file size of most downloaded searches exceeds the capability of most word processors and since askSAM contains many of the same editing capabilities as many

word processors, lately I have been importing directly into
askSAM search strategies, field names, and all.

It is best just to import the existing field names into
askSAM--otherwise, you might have to add them later on.
askSAM can use the imported field names as contextual fields
or you can globally replace them with explicit fields. For
example, CAS Online, one of the STN International databases,
uses TI to designate a title entry, PY to designate publication year, and SO to indicate the name of the source journal.
I can have askSAM sort whatever comes after the PY in reverse
order, and then print out the title, source and year. In one
relatively simply operation, I can combine all the small answer sets into one large answer set sorted by date. If desired, I can do a multiple sort and have the articles
arranged by date and then grouped by the names of the source
journals. This saves the patron time when he or she goes to
retrieve the actual articles.

This procedure works fine with any of the databases
carried by STN International or Medline, and it will also
work with Wilsonline or Dialog files if they are able to be
output with their field tags. As long as there is something
to use as a field name, askSAM can sort on that field. If
there are no field names as with some of the Dialog files,
then searching can be done, and records with the same date
or source or author can be brought together but one cannot
sort unless the desired fields are tagged one by one which
generally is not worth the trouble.

When a search is finished, I pick one of two represen-
tative records and perhaps the search strategy and copy them
into askSAM's memory, and then switch to a file I call
searches and add these few records. I then label them with
the name of the requestor, the date of the search, the amount
of the search, the dept, major professor, account number,
etc. and keep an easily retrievable historical account of all
my past searches. This enables me to quickly review the last
search for any repeat customers, as well as given me materials and statistics for year-end reports.

43

SMALL SCALE SYSTEMS ANALYSIS

Bruce B. Cox
PDL Fellow
Patent Depository Library Program Office
U.S. Patent and Trademark Office

Systems analysts for small scale (microcomputer) applications[1] follow the same rules as those who work on large scale applications. Microanalysis diverges from systems analysis in that essentially one person analyzes a task that can be fully comprehended by that person. The microanalyst will usually rely on the power of database management systems (DBMSs) and other off-the-shelf software in lieu of highly developed programming skills, but more than likely will be thoroughly familiar with the application area.

The essence of systems analysis consists in discovering the skeleton of ideas[2] that are implemented in the current system or formulating the ideas for a new system, and then translating those ideas into automated procedures. Computers are capable, even with the help of sophisticated DBMSs, of a limited range of unit operations, while human activity knows no limit as evidenced in the continued evolution of our society. Arranging the unit operations[3] in such a way as to achieve the desired results demands creativity and compromise, even on the small scale.

Top down microanalysis consists of a series of operations that can be described in six steps:

I. Analyze the workflow of the task to be automated to discover its logic. Microanalysis assumes that the context of the task is well enough defined and understood.

II. Design the user interface (menu tree and input/output screens). The capabilities of the DBMS package used and the requirements of the workflow logic control this operation.

---

[1]Hereafter referred to as "microanalysis." (Defined in Webster's New Collegiate Dictionary, 1974, as "... analysis on a small or minute scale that usually requires special, very sensitive, or small-scale apparatus.")

[2]Most library systems attempt to impose a certain kind of order on the chaos of publications and other information sources we are faced with. The essence of the order imposed is that it be well understood within its cultural context.

[3]Sequence (x then y then z), iteration (repetition of a sequence), conditional (if-then-else), are three common control structures.

III. Design the data structures. Structures which preserve data indepen-
dence (such as the relational model), secure flexibility for future
applications, allowing easy modification.

IV. Design the modules which perform the functions at the ends of the
branches of the menu tree. If the DBMS has an applications generator, coding may not be necessary, or at least will be geatly reduced.
This operation is highly iterative and involves repeated testing of
modules seperately and together.

V. Optimize performance. Most DBMS procedural languages are interpret-
ed, but can be compiled using third party software. In addition, experienced DBMS programmers have discovered coding practices which
will greatly reduce execution time, even without compiling.

VI. Create appropriate documentation. If the user interface is well designed, user documentation can be kept to a minimum. Documentation
for maintenance of the system and future enhancements is another
matter, requiring constant attention and record keeping.

These steps will be illustrated at the Conference through the design of
a general purpose name-address file, and through the design of a union
list of the patent collections of the sixty-two Patent Depository Libraries.

45

SUPPORTING THE "OFF-LINE" DATABASE:
TECHNICAL ISSUES AND THE PROBLEM OF PUBLIC ACCESS
Howard Curtis, Mann Library, Cornell University

Academic libraries have been providing intermediated
search services of online databases for better than a
decade. In recent years, prompted in part by the
appearance of more easily used database search software
systems, many libraries have also begun to teach patrons
to perform their own database searches in "end-user"
training programs.

A major obstacle to the expansion of library support
for online services is the cost of online information
retrieval. At Mann Library, for instance, the amount
spent on searches of commercial, online systems increased
from $12,000 in 1978-79 to $46,100 in 1985-86. Although
the library recovers the bulk of this expense by charging
patrons for search services or by securing subsidies from
College administration for student searches, these costs
still represent the expenditure of "hard dollars" by
individuals or organizations within the university
community. The expense of online searching makes it
impossible for some library patrons to take full advantage
of online information resources.

During the 1980s, computing has witnessed remarkable
advances in the price\performance ratios of processors,
RAM memory, and secondary storage devices. That the
appearance of inexpensive microcomputers has
revolutionized computing is widely acknowledged, while
advances in magnetic disk technology and the emergence of
compact disk and optical disk now permit the storage of
massive amounts of data at reasonable cost.
Unfortunately, the costs of telecommunications and of
producing the information that constitutes online
databases have if anything increased during the same
period. As a result, the searching of commercial online
systems remains, in general, as expensive as ever. While
a microcomputer executing front-end communications
software may simplify life for a person searching an
online system running on a remote computer, it does not
dramatically reduce the costs of a search--macros, offline
query preparation, uploading, and what not
notwithstanding.

One obvious way to eliminate the telecommunications
portion of the online costs equation is to stop searching
on a vendor's remote computer, instead setting up the
database on a local machine under the control of the
library or its university computing center. As is well
known, compact disk already makes this transition possible
for the set of scholarly databases that have begun to be
marketed in this format. Compact disk, of course, suffers

the limitation of being a read-only media. Compact disk is thus a tool useful in the publication and dissemination of databases of general interest; the library or information center cannot modify the contents of a file locally, or easily create a specialized information resource specific to a group of patrons. By contrast, large magnetic disk systems, and, increasingly, optical disk, offer the capability to create custom databases on-site.

In the past year, Mann Library has experimented with both magnetic disk and compact disk as vehicles that allow a library to provide patrons with local access, at no charge, to computerized databases of scholarly information. Because our final goal in both cases has been to establish systems which library patrons, properly prepared, can use without undue reliance on Public Services staff, the project work has involved both (1) evaluating the variety of search-and-retrieval interfaces available from the standpoint of adequacy for the inexperienced searcher, and (2) resolving the technical difficulties in putting together effective hardware and software combinations.

In the first project, funded by grants from the Council on Library Resources, IBM and Cornell University (Project Ezra), and the Office of Research of the College of Agriculture and Life Sciences at Cornell, the library has explored the capabilities of current-generation microcomputers and citation management software for the control of substantial files of bibliographic information. Through a cooperative agreement with the National Agricultural Library, the library secured on magnetic tape a subset of the AGRICOLA database in the subject area of agricultural economics. The subset, consisting of 8,300 citations and approximately 10 megabytes of data in MARC format, was mounted on magnetic disk on a VAX 8500 computer operated by Cornell Computer Services, reformatted to the specifications of a variety of microcomputer-based citation management packages, transferred from mainframe to microcomputer over the campus network, and loaded into the respective database managers. Librarians, working with a set of criteria developed by the Mann Public Services Department, then evaluated the performance of these software packages. The results of our tests will lead to the selection of one package, which will be introduced to undergraduates in the library's end-user search program during spring semester 1987.

The second project focuses on compact disk as a delivery medium for databases of citations and other sources of scholarly information. Here, the library has made an effort to secure, through purchase or by arranging to serve as a "<u>beta</u>" test site, all compact-disk-based databases with potential application in our area of subject responsibility. Public Services' evaluation criteria for compact disk systems differ somewhat from those used in the first project because of the "bound" relationship that exists with compact disk between the data and the search-and-retrieval software. As with our project in magnetic storage technology, the ultimate goal is public access. During spring semester 1987, the library will make two workstations with data files on compact disk available to patrons.

Fee-Based Software Instruction: The Texas A&M Solution

Mel Dodd, Texas A&M University

In 1982 Texas A&M University officials decided to
provide funding for personal computer services to students.
As a result the library expanded its Learning Resources
Department to include personal computers for student and
staff use.   In those beginning days the computers were
Apples; in the following year were added Tandy Radio Shack
Model IIIs, IBM PCs, and other computers.

The Learning Resources Department, or LRD, provided
software as well as computers. These included word processors, spread sheets, and data base managers (or file managers) as well as statistical packages, educational packages,
programming languages and on and on. As time passed,
several different options in the above categories became
available. Evidence mounted that university students and
staff needed help in making good use of the possibilities
afforded them in the LRD.

During this time the Library Director provided the
impetus and the means to bring computing more into the daily
operations of the library staff. She made the library an
enthusiastic participant in the OCLC program. Even more,
she instituted a year long program in computer literacy
engaging a Visiting Professor for a full year; the Professor
was instrumental in bringing the staff to a more or less
friendly relationship with computers and computing.

As time passed the staff appreciated the advantages of
computers more and more. And with this appreciation came a
desire to expand the advantages more widely throughout the
library's work force.

So from the outside and from the inside of the library
grew a need to learn more about the practical uses of
computers. The students needed help -- the staff needed
help. What to do? The library's response was to create a
position, Coordinator for Microcomputer Instruction and
Services, with the responsibility of providing classes in
software use, helping solve or debug computing problems, and
continuing the impetus of the literacy program already
begun.

The Coordinator's responsibilities were directed toward
two audiences: the library staff and the campus users
(mostly students). As the use of computers began to grow
within the library work place, daring replaced caution.

That was good. With the new boldness came "trying things
that didn't work." That was good, too. Still, it elevated
the need for troubleshooting. Along with the new fearless-
ness came a new carelessness. More troubleshooting. So the
Coordinator began to spend time helping staff find out what
went wrong and how to prevent its recurrence.

As the advantages of computers became more obvious to
staff members and their supervisors, the demand for training
in the use of the computer grew. Many wanted classes in
word processing. That meant WordStar for us. Others wanted
to learn how to use a program to retrieve lost or erased
files. There was a need to learn about the new aspects of
hard disks as they became available. Classes were presented. In some instances training took on a one-to-one aspect.

The Coordinator had another job: reviewing software.
This served a two-fold purpose. First, it created a means
of informing staff about new, possibly useful software.
Second, it gave the LRD another person to consider software
that might be of use to other people than library staff.

Campus users especially needed training in the use of
software, particularly some word processing program. After
all, the advantages of a word processor over the typewriter
were quickly obvious to anyone who chanced to look. Some
people had a natural affinity to computing -- they were
eager to get at a computer and play and work and experiment.
But many who wanted the advantages of computing wanted no
part of experimenting and playing -- they wanted to get down
to cases. So while some interest existed in other computer
programs, word processing was in particular demand.

Classes were set up to teach WordStar, a program of
long history, wide use, and low expense. Students are
charged thirty-five dollars for a ten hour class. They are
introduced to the computer and to the operating system, DOS.
They are carried through the WordStar operations in which
they type, edit, do searches for character strings as well
as replacements of character strings. They learn to enhance
the appearance of their printed results by inserting print
control characters into the text. They learn to reformat
their documents, changing margins, spacing, tabs, etc. And
they learn to use dot commands which provide extensive
control over the printing of a document.

The money collected from these courses has been used to
construct a classroom which does not compete with the
remainder of the LRD for space or computers. Now more
classes can be taught with greater flexibility in time and
content. And just in the nick of time. The popularity of
the LRD is growing at a gratifying, almost alarming rate.

ELECTRONIC COMMUNICATIONS IN LIBRARIES:
POSSIBILITIES AND OPTIONS

Rebecca M. Dunkle and William C. Manspeaker,
University of Michigan

In some form electronic communication has been used
in libraries for several years. In what are now
traditional activities, the use of a microcomputer or
terminal to reach major database vendors, or the
dedicated linking of terminals to major bibliographic
utilities, are two examples of how the potential of
electronic communication has been successfully employed
in libraries.

Since these developments and as more and more
libraries began acquiring equipment, especially
microcomputers, for this type of communication, more
opportunities and options have become available.

On the national level, major electronic bulletin
board systems such as Compuserve and The Source allow
users to share information directly. Library-specific
options are the American Library Association's ALANET,
which allows members to receive up-to-date information
quickly and share information with colleagues through
personal messages, and the recently formed Library
Microcomputer Users' Group. Librarians are also able to
take advantage of disciplineoriented electronic
communication, such as ScholarNet, an electronic service
that currently offers the opportunity to communicate with
colleagues in two divisions: HumaNet, (English, history,
philosophy and religion) and PoliNet (political science,
public administration, and criminal justice.)

Libraries are beginning to adapt this technology
locally to enhance direct services to users, using
electronic mail, bulletin board systems, and/or online
conferencing. At the University of Michigan, patrons are
able to take advantage of the library's online reference
services to send requests to the reference department
through the campus-wide electronic message system, and
receive responses the same way; a document delivery
service, through which books and articles requested by
electronic mail are delivered directly to the faculty;
and online distribution of database search results to the
patron's electronic mailbox.

APPLE LIBRARY USERS GROUP

Monica Ertel, Apple Computer, Inc.

The **Apple Library Users Group (ALUG)** was begun in 1981 as a forum for librarians, media specialists and information professionals to share information with one another about their use of Apple computers. From a small beginning of 35 members in 1981, this users group has grown to over 8,000 members from around the world, including the People's Republic of China. The main method of communication of ALUG is a quarterly newsletter which contains information on the latest products from Apple, software and hardware reviews by members, an active question and answer column and many articles about what members are doing with their Apple computers. The **ALUG Newsletter** was awarded "The Best Newsletter from a Corporation" by John Dvorak from InfoWorld.

ALUG also sponsors the **Apple Library Template Exchange** which is a cooperative effort on the part of ALUG members to share with one another solutions to common problems. Anyone who has applied a database manager or a spreadsheet to a particular task has had first to format the entry screens and then determine the print routines. It is the initial "set-up" of a database or a spreadsheet that makes those programs a bit intimidating to the new or first-time user or just time-consuming for the experienced user. The Template Exchange is useful for both groups. The Template Exchange currently has over 200 templates for AppleWorks as well as about 50 PFS templates, DB Master, dbase II and assorted other programs. Macintosh templates are also available through the Template Exchange.

The **Apple Library Users Group** has their annual meeting once a year at the American Library Association Annual Conference. The meetings consist of an annual report on the year's activities of ALUG, a presentation from Apple management including a question and answer period, and discussion groups on topics such as "*Software Circulation*", "*Telecommunications*", "*Public Access*", "*Computer Literacy*" and more. This year's meeting will be held during ALA's San Francisco conference on July 1.

Membership in ALUG is free. For more information, write to Apple Library Users Group, 10381 Bandley Drive, MailStop 8C, Cupertino, CA 95014 or call 408/973-2552.

The **Apple Library Users Group** meeting to be held at SCIL will focus on new products from Apple as well as provide time for attendees to talk to one another about their use of computers in their particular libraries or information centers.

LIBRARY AUTOMATION AT A MULTI-CAMPUS COMMUNITY COLLEGE

Deirdre A. Farris
Systems and Computer Technology Corporation

Viveca Yoshikawa
Hillsborough Community College
Tampa, Florida

A new solution to the charge of automating libraries on a limited budget! Hillsborough Community College will present how they converged technologies to meet their automation objectives. The system utilizes a VAX 11/780, IBM PCXTs and MS-DOS software. Running micro software on a VAX? We will tell you how we do it. The laser disc-based BiblioFile is used for retrospective conversion and current cataloging. The Ocelot Library System is used to searched the catalog, to circulate books and to do acquisitions. Following a description of this system, a discussion of considerations, implications and suggested guidelines for library automation projects will be presented.

AN INTEGRATED LIBRARY SYSTEM : HELP FOR THE SMALL LIBRARY

Denise Fesmire & Joanne Guyton, Methodist Hospitals of Memphis

The Leslie M. Stratton Nursing Library serves a student body ranging from two hundred (200) to four hundred fifty (450) students, the School of Nursing faculty and administration, the Division of Nursing which includes eight hundred fifty (850) nurses and related associates, and all other associates of the system except physicians who are served by the medical library. Circulation in 1980 ran about 12,000 items. By 1984 this had more than doubled. Staff included three (3) FTE's, two librarians and a clerical person, plus student assistants who worked night and weekend hours. An increase in services to the system precipitated the need for either more staff or a more efficient way to handle the procedures related to circulation. Since additional staff was out of the question, the possibility of going to an online circulation system was explored.

In July 1984 the school administration announced that money was available for purchase of a microcomputer and software for circulation. The catch was that the money had to be encumbered within two months for both hardware and software. The hospital mandated purchase of IBM hardware. The Sydney Micro Library System was selected although it was still several months from being ready for the market. Three modules were purchased. These were Cataloging/Inquiry, Circulation, and MARC Interface.

The Cataloging/Inquiry module provides the database. There are six (6) programs in this module - add/modify catalog, authority, and inventory data, bar code linking, inquiry, and print reports. Reports include printing labels batch mode or individually, printing bibliographies, catalogs, inventory reports, and authority term reports. Since most of the library's records were on tape at Marcive, they were sent to Sydney for conversion to floppy disks. Once copied to the library's hard disk, they were converted using parameters chosen from the MARC record options on Sydney. Editing of these records began in December 1985. At the same time, records were entered for which the staff had done the original cataloging. When school opened in August 1986, online circulation began. Approximately 6,000 records were edited and/or entered in seven months.

The Circulation module includes programs for front desk activities, maintaining charge code and patron data, printing patron notices and occasional reports, and period end procedures. Patron data was input for over six hundred (600) patrons who had current registration cards. Cards were typed and barcoded for these patrons.

During the time that retrospective records were being edited and entered, the MARC Interface module could not be used to retrieve new records from Marcive. Now that editing and entry of retrospective records is complete, catalog records are being retrieved online from Marcive. No more than twenty (20) records are sent to Marcive at one time. The LC number, title, and holdings information are entered. The requests are sent to Marcive one day and retrieved the following day. If the record is on the Marcive database, the full catalog record is retrieved to be edited. The record corresponds to the library's Marcive profile and the conversion table set up on the Sydney system.

Preplanning is the key to successful changeover to an automated system. This can be difficult since there is no way of knowing all of the changes that will be required until the new system is in operation. One example of a change that caused problems for the Nursing Library staff is the overdue procedure. With the new system, it was not feasible to send overdues daily. Not only the procedure but the policy for overdues had to be changed to use the program effectively.

The fast-paced, high pressure environment has made it difficult to find time to write procedures to use in training students on the system. Some are comfortable using the computer and the system within a short time; others have never completely adjusted to it.

Having a single-user system instead of a network poses several problems. Since the library uses the system primarily for circulation, all activities must be performed at the circulation desk. Interruptions cause mistakes in data entry. Using the system for these procedures also means that circulation must be handled manually, then entered later. Reorganization and period end procedures take several hours and must be run overnight or on weekends. For some of the student assistants this has been a problem.

The Sydney Micro Library System is a sophisticated integrated system with many more capabilities than were anticipated. At this point there has not been time to fully explore all the capabilities. The support provided by Sydney has been very satisfactory. For those with some experience using microcomputers, the system is user-friendly. Help programs are extensive. Those with limited computer experience will have more difficulty. Future plans of the Nursing Library call for networking and for providing terminals for public use.

Flower 1

FULL FEATURED MS/PC-DOS COMPUTING ON THE MOVE

Eric S. Flower, University of Maine

The first of the full featured transportable microcomputers combining a powerful operating system with equally
powerful application software ran under CP/M. Later developments in this field have been primarily in the MS/PC-DOS
arena. These transportables offered the user an opportunity
to have the full complement of features of his or her desktop
with some measure of portability. More recently we have
witnessed the development of full featured microcomputers
characterized by much lower weight and smaller size than the
transportables. They generally support battery operation and
come in a self-contained chassis. They have evolved into
two distinct groups, the portables, which are about the size
of lunch boxes or table radios, and the laptops, which are
briefcase sized. All are characterized by having at least
one disk drive, either 3 1/2" or 5 1/4", a screen, a keyboard, memory capability of 512 to 640K, provisions for an
internal modem, and serial and parallel ports, all in one
cabinet. They are self contained units for the most part.
Today there are more than thirty five companies selling
transportable, portable, or laptop MS/PC-DOS microcomputers.

GUIDELINES FOR SELECTION

With all those machines on the market, how can you make
a sensible decision when selecting a portable?

USE: This is always the first general consideration.
What do you want to do, how, and why? More specifically,
what software will be used, by whom, under what circum-
stances, and at what locations?

PORTABILITY: Will there be frequent or infrequent
moves? Will they be short distances or long hauls? Where
will the computer go?

COMPATIBILITY: We may assume the machine will run the
galaxy of programs written for the IBM-PC/XT. More practical-
ly, it must run the software you and your institution use
today and also the software you will be using tomorrow. Try
the machine with any software or hardware you must have.

CAPABILITY: Can the machine be equipped to do what you
need now and into the foreseeable future or is it a closed
architecture?

56

Flower 2

DURABILITY/SERVICE: Can the machine take it? Sooner or later it will fail. Expect some downtime. Know beforehand what you will do.

INTERFACE: There are two problems here, the screen and the keyboard. At this point in time you will be trading off some features of both. Look at the display and try the keyboard before you buy. There is no way to work around either of them.

DATA TRANSFERABILITY/SOFTWARE LIABILITY: How will you move data between the portable and your other equipment? Implicit in the problem of data transfer is the legal obligation you may incur with the software used to create your data.

BATTERY LIFE: Most of these machines offer rechargeable battery operation. Find out how long they will last from the technical specifications and then ask a user for his experience.

PRINTERS: Printers have become add-ons or completely separate components. All are characterized by small size, low weight, and optional AC or battery operation. Two acceptable printers, at either ends of the price range, may be the $479 Diconix Inkjet 150 and the OnTheGo printer from Laptopp Systems at $150.

Having said all of that, use a little common sense. Your task is to combine these criteria with price to create a value ratio which offers the best combination of features and cost for your needs.

FUTURE TRENDS

Portables, like virtually all other computers in the past, will follow the generalization of more power and storage with increased reliabilty for less money. There will be a convergence of desktop and portable computing power. Two hardware paths appear to lead to the future. The first is to add more and more features into a smaller and smaller case through miniaturization while the second is to add features in modules that may be added or removed as necessary. Miniaturization may be thought of as more of the same. Under modular architecture the system is composed of connecting pieces which may be assembled or disassembled as needed.

More importantly, the portables themselves will be increasingly incorporated into the institutional environment. Look for ever increasing connectivity as the next big development. Future hardware and software developments for portable microcomputers no doubt will be aimed at this market.

INTERFACING VENDOR PACKAGES: A CASE STUDY

Gloria Fulton, Humboldt State University

Executive Summary

The decision to acquire a 3-Com local area network, running on IBM-compatible Leading Edges, for the Humboldt State University Library in May of 1985 was the result of months of investigation and the harbinger of a number of hoped-for benefits: centralization and local control of library computing, future flexibility for software development, a stimulus for the professional staff to develop applications. Two immediate networked applications, word processing and electronic mail, were immediately pressed into service; and Pro-Search and SuperCalc3 (standalone applications) were added soon thereafter. However, the availability of considerable storage space, plus the desire to add some "sexy" features to the system, was the catalyst that caused all of us to examine areas under our collective purview for further possibilities.

As Chair of the Catalog/Serials Department, I was becoming acutely conscious of the need to "do something" about our serials control situation. One critical and limiting factor here was space, money was another, and staffing was yet a third. As we reached the point where new check-in cabinets would have to be ordered, and with no space in which to put them, the advantages of an automated check-in system suddenly seemed overwhelmingly seductive. Several microcomputer-based systems were investigated and compared, with none of them offering all the features we wanted. They either required expensive or extraneous hardware, or the software was out of our budget. We also lacked staffing to build a database.

Around the beginning of 1986, due to a quantity purchase of microcomputers for in-house use, we had an overnight population explosion of Leading Edges (IBM-compatible computers) in the Library, all to be connected to the central 3-Com network server. Suddenly it became both feasible and desirable to place a Leading Edge in the Serials Office. This possibility gave impetus to more serious consideration of a system new on the market, the Faxon MicroLinx serials control system. This system possessed a number of features that were immediately attractive: relatively low software cost, including initial database load of all of our Faxon titles; Faxon bibliographic and systems support; and the possibility that the system might run on a Leading Edge. This possibility led to a further possibility--that the system might be able to run on a network volume that could be accessed from other LE stations in the building.

Of course the sales literature put out by Faxon said nothing about whether any of these possibilities were realistic. However, after some telephone discussion between our Faxon sales rep and our in-house computer consultant, it was agreed that we could "test" a demonstration version on our network. From that test we concluded that the software would run on a compatible, although we were still unsure as to whether we could have shared access from the LAN. It was at this point that I was glad that I had electronic mail, as it affords me the ability to track some of the ups and downs of our communications with the vendor.

Among the problems encountered with the vendor in the acquisition process were the following:

1. Resistance from Faxon to selling the program to an institution which planned to run the software on non-IBM hardware.

2. Refusal to face the issue of its functionality from a remote hard disk.

3. Refusal to speculate on the program's simultaneous accessibility from multiple users granted read-only access.

4. Nonavailability of multi-user version of the program for 3-Com network.

5. Claim that Novell network would not be compatible with 3-Com network, with no plans for development for 3-Com network.

6. Lack of clarification as to whether the multi-user version would run on a network with a dedicated server (such as ours) without a dedicated "database server."

7. Possibility that MicroLinx's interrupt settings might conflict with those used by the microcomputer card used for accessing the remote disk.

Further problems were encountered in the implementation phase, among them chiefly the following:

1. Slower than optimal processing speed.

2. Difficulty in estimating the time required to input non-Faxon titles, causing the database loading to be more time-consuming than anticipated.

3. Write access required for read-only users to get into the program.

4. Faxon's transmission is asynchronous, not synchronous like most standard modems (e.g., Hayes compatibles), so users must usually buy a new modem.

5. Problems with getting the modem to work once installed.

6. Problems with dedicated phone lines for electronic communication.

7. Problems with corrupting the database during simultaneous access.

8. Our network operating system does not support shared volumes with data integrity.

9. Faxon has not yet indicated an interest in testing MicroLinx on a 3-Com network.

In spite of these difficulties, and in hope of eventually surmounting many of them, the system is becoming operational, and will (we hope) result in a system superior in many respects to the old manual one.

THE UNIX/XENIX ADVANTAGE: APPLICATIONS IN LIBRARIES

Kelly L. Gordon, Central Michigan University

Since 1983, the Central Michigan University Libraries
have been committed to the Xenix operating system
environment to support administrative office automation.
Generally included in the library's administrative
automation are five functions: word processing and text
editing, spreadsheets, data base management systems,
electronic mail and communications.   Additional
capabilities such as calendar management and
business graphics enhance the system.   This paper will
discuss the specific applications that the Xenix system has
had in the library and the merits of such an operating
system.

When justifying the purchase of a Unix/Xenix system,
often the advantages and disadvantages are weighed against
the installation of CP/M or MS-DOS based local area
networks.   This was the case at Central Michigan University
where the library faced major opposition from on-campus
groups over the commitment to a Xenix based system.
Arguments against the purchase of a Unix/Xenix system
include:

1)   Unix/Xenix operating systems are not user
friendly.

2)   There are non-standard versions.

3)   DOS, and IBM machines and look-a-likes are more
standard, whereas there has been no 'hit' computer (a
big seller) that relies on Unix as its' operating
system.
4)   Applications software is limited when compared to
the number of packages that run on DOS.

5)   IBM/compatibles may already be in place and staff
may already be familiar with DOS.

6)   On a local area network, each work station can be
used as a personal computer whereas a Unix/Xenix
system uses dumb terminals as workstations.

The truth is that Unix/Xenix is a very special operating
system.   It is extremely complicated and powerful.   It is
not as unfriendly as many suggest and there are hundreds of
applications packages available, many of them menu driven.
"It is not a manufacture's system, steeped in hardware

61

dependence, neither is it limited in application - it is an ideal system for writing, programming and communications. It is easily the most complete operating system in existence today." (Fiedler & Hunter, 1986).

While the above testimonial ranks a bit strong, the continued commitment to the Xenix operating system on the part of the Central Michigan University Libraries is based on the satisfaction and contentment that we are headed in the right direction. Given the administrative and office automation functions in our library environment, the following advantages of a Xenix operating system have been realized:

1) The capacity to accommodate particular needs. Each user can view the system from their own perspective and the user environment can be taylored to meet the sophistication of the individual. Some users may need detailed menus while others prefer to operate in the various Xenix shells.

2) The ability to flexibly share files. Users may access files simultaneously. Flexible control of permissions to files allows project groups to access common files while denying access to others.

3) The ability to share peripherals. Several users can share a single printer or modem, thus greater economy without sacrificing flexibility.

4) Centralized system administration. Staff can utilize the system without worrying about ruining diskettes, making backups or even turning off the machine. Floppy disks are virtually eliminated saving time and footsteps.

5) The cost of software is minimized and resides on the machine where legally purchased by license agreement.

The initial Xenix system developed from the need to extend single user Radio Shack equipment to more users in the library. By adding expansion boards, hard disks, dumb terminals and Xenix software, the library expanded a single user microcomputer to nine work stations on a multi-user system. The library has realized such advantages from the multi-user environment that it has installed three larger and more powerful Xenix systems on Altos hardware; two Altos 986 clusters capable of accommodating eight users each and an Altos 2086, serving fifteen users. One of the Altos 986 clusters is installed in an off-campus library in

62

Virginia. (Figure 1). The impending addition of network
software will interconnect Xenix clusters, allowing all
resources on the systems to be accessed as though combined
into a single file system.

The installation of the Xenix operating system at the
Central Michigan University Libraries has propelled
librarians into the information age. It was a primary
administrative objective to provide librarians computer
capabilities for the support of scholarship and
publication. With the Xenix system, librarians can now
perform database searching, use a word processor for
correspondence, access a powerful visual editor useful in
creating and sorting serials lists, generate monthly
statistics with a spread sheet and illustrate them using
business graphics; all without leaving the terminal on his
or her desk. (figure 2). The library has become self
sufficient, lessened our dependence on campus computer
services and automated document delivery and office
procedures with sophisticated database management systems.

Reference

Fiedler, D. and Hunter, B.H. (1986). UNIX System
Administration. Hasbrouck Heights, New Jersey: Hayden.

Figure 1

XENIX SYSTEM CONFIGURATION

2ND FLOOR

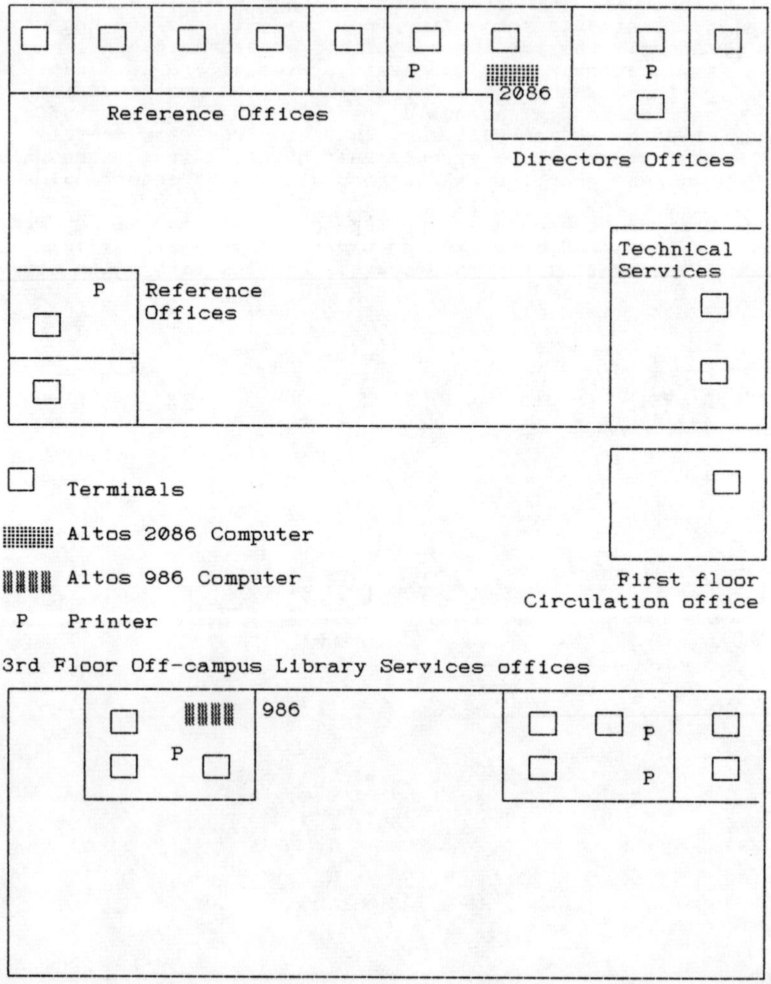

Reference Offices

2086

Directors Offices

Reference
Offices

Technical
Services

☐ Terminals

▦ Altos 2086 Computer

▥ Altos 986 Computer

P   Printer

First floor
Circulation office

3rd Floor Off-campus Library Services offices

986

Figure 2

Menu Driven Applications

CALENDARS	WORD PROCESSING
Calendar Manager Delete Calendar List Calendars	Edit document Print document Mail Merge Delete Document Word Processing Menu
ELECTRONIC MAIL	COMMUNICATIONS
Electronic Mail Who is on the system Enable/disable messages Send to all users Enable/Disable Messages	Async Communication Wait for file transfer

GRAPHICS	DATABASE
Business Graphics Delete Graphs List Graphs	Informix Enter data Make database queries Print report to file Print report to printer
SPREADSHEET	
Multiplan Print Spreadsheet Merge with Transfer File Delete spreadsheet	

THE KANSAS STATE UNIVERSITY LIBRARIES'
MICROCOMPUTER/MAINFRAME SERIALS LISTS

Charlene Grass, Kansas State University Libraries

KSU Libraries currently maintains and updates two
serials lists on microcomputer. The first contains records
for 33,000+ active and dead serial titles. The second
reflects only currently received serial titles. Both lists
are accommodated on a Zenith 200 microcomputer (AT
compatible) with 512K and 20 MB hard disk storage. The
lists are accessed through a common menu which leads to
editing programs written using dBase III. During the summer
and fall of 1986, KSU's University Computing completed the
programming according to library specifications.

Comprehensive Serials List

Each record in this list is composed of the following
fields: Control no.; Date of Change to record; ISSN; OCLC
no.; Title/Description (150 characters); No. of lines in
Title/Description field; Call no. The Title/Description
Field is parsed by line into: (a) title; (b) summary holding
information; (c) specific location holding information.

The structure of this list is somewhat odd due the fact
that the data comprising it formerly resided in a mainframe
maintained database file which featured no true field
designations. Logical subdivision of data was accomplished
via mainframe data processing to produce fielded records
suitable for control via dBase. Thus re-entry of data was
avoided.

A notable feature of the new microcomputer based
database is the piecing together of long Title/Description
Fields from smaller records held in multiple database files
(.DBF) thus avoiding the limit of 254 characters while not
assigning "empty" space in the majority of records which do
not exceed the dBase limit.

Custom editing procedures are used with this database
and native dBase commands cannot be used to manipulate the
database. Key word searching and searches of other fields
are provided. KSU is considering placing a copy of this
list at Reference to be used for such searching.

The final product of this list is a widely distributed
version produced on microfiche. The fiche vendor requires a
standard magnetic tape containing the formatted listing. At
this time it was not considered economically viable to
attach a tape drive to a microcomputer; and, further, it is
uncertain whether dBase could use such a drive. Procedures
were written to periodically upload changes to the
microcomputer-based list via the KERMIT communications

package to the University's mainframe. Programs for incorporating changes and producing a formatted COM ready tape are executed on the mainframe using a tape archived version of the list.

The date of change to a record assumes extreme importance as the sort element deciding which portions of the micro database are uploaded, thus avoiding uploading the entire database. A crucial feature in this scheme is careful planning for synchronization of these duplicate databases. For, example, deletions are not really processed in the micro database until a printout of the changes as uploaded and incorporated into the mainframe resident database is examined.

The Comprehensive Serials List pushes the microcomputer and dBase to its limits. It is seen as an interim measure. It is hoped that the holdings data in this database can someday be transferred to an integrated library system and attached to a bibliographic record via the connecting link of the OCLC no.--thus, again, avoiding total data reentry.

Serials Cost List

This simpler list of 9000+ serial titles currently received is composed of records with the following elements: Call no.; Location; ISSN; OCLC no.; Fund Code; Purchase type(periodical, standing order, exchange, etc.); Vendor; Country of publication; Copies; Title; Cost for current year and three past years; Percentage increase of cost.

Native dBase commands are used with the Cost List to produce sorts and printouts according to various mixes of variables in the records. This information is used in collection development and budgeting decisions.

Administrative Comments

In completing these projects, the Libraries were required to use microcomputer obtained as part of a state-wide contract. This model was not in general use and has since been discontinued. We have experienced numerous breakdowns--which reveals a hidden danger in state contracts which do not require that only equipment already field operational be bid.

The Libraries' experience also shows that it is still true that requirements of such projects must be carefully spelled out to university data processing; that delays are to be expected from typically overburdened university computing centers and that getting full documentation from a programmer may still be likened to pulling hen's teeth.

USING TEXT RETRIEVAL SOFTWARE FOR A
DO-IT-YOURSELF ONLINE CATALOG

James Hambleton, Texas State Law Library

By integrating several inexpensive off-the-shelf software packages, the Texas State Law Library has created a
microcomputer based on-line catalog of newer titles that
may be searched simultaneously by users in the library and
by those dialing in on their own terminals.

The process starts with library staffers dialing into
RLIN on search-only accounts. Hits are downloaded to a hard
disk, from which they are later pulled up and edited. Cataloging data is then electronically "cut" from these edited
RLIN records, and electronically "pasted" into the tagged
fields of a catalog card production program called Ultracard.

Ultracard writes this data into ASCII text files.
These ASCII text files are used by Ultracard to produce
headed card sets, book and pocket labels, and acquisitions lists. The acquisitions list module can be configured to print out records by main entry, by call number,
by author or by subject.

The next step is to take these Ultracard-produced ASCII
text files and run them against a text retrieval program.
The retrieval program the library uses, FYI 3000+, does not
require data to be in tagged fields. Rather, the program
treats each cataloging record as one entry. When each entry
is indexed, then, there is no distinction about whether a
particular word is an author, title, or subject word.

The result is that when searches are performed in this
on-line catalog, hits are retrieved much the same way as
they are in full text retrieval systems such as LEXIS or
WESTLAW. Entering the word "tort" will retrieve a cataloging record if the book were written by Joe Tort, issued by
the ABA Section of Tort Law, or if the record contained the
subject heading "tort". This particular program also offers
full truncation and boolean searching.

In addition to offering the text retrieval program, the
FYI people are testing an electronic bulletin board designed
to work with the text retrieval program. The bulletin board
program provides all the "regular" features of such software, such as electronic mail, "chat" boards, as well as
general files where information that can be downloaded is
posted. The State Law Library posts its monthly acquisitions
list (which was generated by Ultracard) as one of the general files for people to browse through or to download.

Along with these features, the bulletin board software

provides a window into the text retrieval program. That is,
people dialing in can search the library's catalog using the
same features (truncation and boolean logic) that are available to a user of the text retrieval program in the library.

The last step in implementing the on-line catalog was
to take one microcomputer and chop its processing power in
two so that it could be used simultaneously by someone in
the library and someone dialing in. The library runs a
program called DoubleDos which does just that. DoubleDos
splits up the microprocessor's computing power, allowing
each program a few nanoseconds to do what it is supposed to
do. For users of the bulletin board, the fact that the
micro is running under DoubleDos is transparent. However,
search time for the user of the on-line catalog in the
library is noticeably slowed.

Without DoubleDos an average search is about five to
ten seconds; under DoubleDos this time increases twofold.
The advantage of running DoubleDos is that one micro does
not have to be dedicated to running the bulletin board.
When the price of oil (and with it funding for Texas state
agencies) rises, the library plans to buy a micro to dedicate to the bulletin board. The FYI people are also testing
a board that will allow access by eight telephone callers at
once.

While glitches have cropped up in using the on-line
system, and satisfactory documentation for its use has yet
to be written, the cost of implementing the system has been
minimal. The text retrieval software is licensed free of
charge, as is the bulletin board software, and the amount of
staff time for the project has been slight. The data used
for the system is data captured in the normal library
routine to produce catalog cards.

Since the State Law Library only has a staff of seven,
which includes its three professional librarians, there is
no retrospective conversion project. The on-line catalog
only contains titles cataloged within the last two years
(the period of time Ultracard has been used.) There are
currently about 1,800 records in the system.

The on-line catalog at the State Law Library is viewed
as a by-product of the "real" card catalog, not as its
replacement. Data captured to create catalog cards is simply dumped into the on-line catalog with no further editing.
The amount of time needed to update the on-line catalog is
about 20 minutes a month. Data captured once, then, does
the double duty of maintaining a conventional card catalog
and building an on-line catalog for the future.

MICROCOMPUTERS IN THE GOVERNMENT DOCUMENTS DEPARTMENT

Tony A. Harvell, University of Miami Library

Government documents departments in libraries often function as a microcosm of the library as a whole. These departments often select, order, catalog, process, and circulate their own materials, as well as provide reference assistance for their collections. Microcomputers can be used to assist with many of these functions. Most government documents departments maintain various files that would be quite adaptable to microcomputer operations. These files are frequently quite cumbersome, and may require multiple access points. We have begun applying microcomputers to the operations described below in the Government Publications Department at the University of Miami Libraries. Since many documents departments would have similar requirements, we would like to share our experience.

We maintain a separate circulation file for materials circulated from our reference desk. We had used a file of multiple forms with two access points (patron name and call number). This file had become quite large over the years as our circulations increased. We were finding it more difficult to develop a mechanism to alert us to send overdue notices in a timely fashion. Our first project using the microcomputer was to input our circulation records into a text-oriented data management system. We chose AskSam produced by Seaside Software in Corpus Christi, Texas. Although we still must manually input all of the checkout forms, we find this package to be extremely useful in allowing us to generate printouts by patron name and by call number, as well as generate overdue notices on a regular basis. Although we cannot dedicate our microcomputer entirely to circulation, we find we are able to set aside certain periods for a student assistant to work on circulation file maintenance.

We have also converted our "want list" file of missing issues of periodicals using the AskSam package. This file was quite cumbersome and suffered from inconsistencies of entry. We find that by using AskSam we can update it easily and can also produce a print product to send to the Superintendent of Documents for their "Needs and Offers Lists." This package could also be used by selective depositories to send their "disposition lists" to the regional or other selective depositories in their state.

One of our most recent projects is a union list of major government documents sets in Florida libraries. Once again, using AskSam, we have produced a questionnaire and union list using the same set of bibliographic records.

This format lends itself well to updating and various
manipulations of the information it contains.

Documents departments will be receiving more
information in machine readable form. Presently we are
receiving data from the Bureau of Economic Analysis on
diskette. Documents librarians can prepare for this
technology by familiarizing themselves with various
statistical software packages that may be used with
government statistical data. Recent discussions at
meetings of the Depository Library Council indicate that
more government information will be distriubted in this
format, including both statistical and textual information.

Our experience leads us to make the following
suggestions to documents departments considering applying
microcomputers to their operations. Carefully consider
which files might be converted to machine-readable form.
Be aware of any limitations in capabilities of equipment or
software packages before converting files. Prepare your own
documentation as you go along, if necessary. Always make
backup copies of files on a continual basis. Keep informed
of how libraries have successfully undertaken these
projects. It may be possible to use another library's
programming or data files and save considerable duplication
of efforts. One very useful source of information is
Administrative Notes from the Library Programs Service of
the Government Printing Office. The "Readers Exchange"
columns of recent issues have contained informative
descriptions of successful applications of microcomputers in
documents departments. Library networks and other
organizations often sponsor useful workshops on
microcomputer applications. College and university campuses
frequently offer classes at little or no cost to users. It
is important to keep your library administrators informed of
successful microcomputer applications. This is
particularly important when making equipment requests.
Above all, it is important to communicate with your
colleagues through informal microcomputer users groups in
the library. Keep informed of new technologies through the
literature. Finally, remember that the possibilities for
microcomputer applications in government publications are
limited only by equipment availability and imagination.

Developing the Hardware and Software
for a
Statewide Referral Database

J. J. Hayden III, Southeastern Library Network

The Indiana Youth Resources Information Network (IYRIN)
project produced and distributed a reference database system to
15 public libraries in Indiana. These libraries had widely varying amounts of computer experience. This paper deals with the
selection criteria used for system hardware and software as well
as with the particulars of the software systems design and implementation. A review of the expectations compared to the actual functioning of the systems in the field is included in the
scope of this paper. The developmental evolution of the system
software is also discussed.

The basic design goal was to provide a computer based
reference database that could be maintained by staff at the participating libraries, and that could provide necessary data. The
production of a statewide file composed of the fifteen individual
files was most easily accomplished by using the same database
software at each site. The desire to provide a computer based
system that could be supported locally could have been met by
using any of several types of computer systems, but the PC
"standard" microcomputer was chosen in part because PC type computers give the participating libraries a general purpose tool in
addition to a reference database system. The need to simultaneously update and access the database necessitated multiple
access points to the database. A Local Area Network (LAN) that
uses PCs as the workstations was chosen because the network system software provides multiple access and yet also control the
simultaneous use of files. The final link in the system was the
statewide collection and distribution of data. Although each
system was equipped with a modem and telecommunications software,
the expense of transmitting large amounts of data--1.5 to 2.5
million characters--over the telephone lines was prohibitive. A
system that allows data to be loaded onto cartridge discs which
are shipped to a central site and merged into the state database,
which, in turn, is placed back onto the cartridge, and
redistributed to the libraries has provided a cost effective system.

The design of the database, that is, what information would
be in the database was the most critical aspect of the IYRIN system. Ms B. J. Whitaker of INCOLSA has dealt with the particulars
of this most difficult task in her paper. The structure of the
database had an impact on the structure of the software and vice
versa. The first decision concerned the degree of involvement
with the workings of the database that would be required of the
staff in participating libraries. If each library were provided
with a general purpose database system and the format of the
database, then there would have to be a database expert at each
library. In fact there would have had to be several experts so
that the availability of the data would not depend on the
presence of a particular person. A database--dBase III Plus--

72

that could be used to produce menu driven applications systems, was selected. In order to assist in the task of supporting fifteen systems, the dBase programs were compiled and linked together so that the same database programs are distributed to each library.

The design of the programs that make up the IYRIN system was guided by the requirements of individuals who had been providing reference services. This direct input by the people who are actually using the system is probably the most important element in its production. Several design goals were established:

The data entry would be from questionnaires, and should be arranged so that the programs requested the data in the order that it is found on the questionnaire.

The data stored in the database fell into two types, a set of fixed length fields, and a set of variable length fields.

Some fixed and variable length fields are mandatory, and others are optional.

Some of the data would be validated against control files prior to its addition to the master file.

Search and report programs can use several of the fields to retrieve information from the database.

Searches can be modified by subsequent searches to produce reports and displays of data.

The ERIC descriptors were used as the thesaurus.

Countys, cities, townships, ZIP codes, and regions are entered into a controlled vocabulary list to provide geographic access points.

The IYRIN system has a complete edit/verify/update system in addition to the normal search/report system. Before new or modified data becomes part of the online database, the data must pass a verification procedure. This is done to ensure the accuracy of the system.

The IYRIN system has presented several challenges and opportunities. The use of PCs, LANs, and dBase to produce a distributed statewide database has been a rewarding endeavor to a large extent because of the dedication of the people from the libraries and library support organizations.

DBASE III FOR ACQUISITIONS DEPARTMENT BUDGETS
Lynne Meyers Hayman, Beaver College

This paper describes materials budget allocation to academic departments by a small college library. The Atwood Library of Beaver College runs dBase III Plus on an IBM PC M300 with a 20 mg. hard disk.

In the 1985-86 academic year, the library director of the Atwood Library of Beaver College decided to refine the process of allocating its materials budget to academic departments, by distributing the cost of subscriptions. Traditionally, a portion of the materials budget had been set aside at the beginning of each academic year to cover the cost of serials subscriptions. Remaining funds were then allocated to academic departments for book purchases. Because, in recent years, the materials budget has not grown proportionately with increases in subscription costs, fewer funds were available for book purchases each year. An increasing percentage of the materials budget was devoted to the library's 645 subscriptions.

Employing dBase to assign the cost of subscriptions, as well as books, to academic departments, has enabled the library to more accurately monitor the real share of the materials budget claimed by each academic department. It has also made possible the reassignment of funds to a department for additional book purchases or subscriptions, when the department initiates a subscription cancellation.

In designing the system, two database files of active periodical titles and continuations were initially created. Subscription prices were included for each title. Each title was also assigned one or more department codes based on its subject content. The report form function of dBase was used to generate reports for all departments of relevant titles and subscription costs. No additional programming was required to produce these reports. Reports were distributed to departmental chairs, who were asked to indicate which titles were, indeed, relevant to their disciplines.

When all reports were returned to the library, the databases were updated to appropriately delete departmental codes. Revised reports were then produced and distributed. If a title had been shared by two departments in the first report distribution and had been rejected by one department, the other department was asked to indicate in the second report distribution whether it wished to assume the full cost of the journal. Based on resposes, reports were revised and distributed several times. When the process was completed, those titles which had not been claimed were proposed for cancellation. When a subscription was cancelled, the funds became available to the department for book purchases or new subscriptions.

74

Now, at the beginning of each new subscription period, prices are updated in the database file, and new reports are distributed to departmental chairs for review.

In addition to files of periodical titles and continuations, another database file was created to store data on departmental materials budgets. Each record in the file includes fields for department code, periodicals committment, continuations committment, book budget, and total departmental budget. A program was written, which supplies figures in the periodicals and continuations committment fields by processing the database files of periodical titles and continuations coded by department. At the beginning of each fiscal year, sums are assigned to departments for book purchases after serials committments have been subtracted from the materials budget. These figures are entered in the book budget field of each record. The total departmental budget is the sum of serials committments and share of the book budget. If a department initiates a new periodical subscription, the cost is added to periodical committments, and the departmental book budget is decreased proportionately. Similarly, if a subscription is cancelled, if it changes price or is assigned to a different department, committment figures are updated to reflect these changes; and the departmental book budget is adjusted to reflect an appropriate increase or decrease.

After these serials modules were designed, they were linked to the library's book acquisitions system, also designed and programmed in dBase. When changes in a department's serials committments result in an adjustment to the book budget figure, this revised figure is transferred to the book acquisitions system, where book order committments and invoices are subtracted from the book budget to maintain a record of available funds.

NOTABLE MICROCOMPUTER SOFTWARE AND HARDWARE IN ACADEMIA:

THE STATE OF COLLECTIONS TODAY

OR,

282 SHOPPING DAYS 'TIL CHRISTMAS

Anne Hess, California State University, Los Angeles

A year ago, 282 days before Christmas, I went shopping--
for notable collections of microcomputer software and
hardware in academia.

My comments will relate primarily to my discoveries
about 6 collections. These are general-access collections
featuring more than 1 brand of microcomputer. Four of the
collections are located in and managed by libraries. The
other 2 collections are located within library buildings but
are managed by academic computing services.

I will refer to these collections mainly as "labs." I
will use primarily present tense; however, most of the data
was presented to me last summer--the summer of '86.

Below is a sampling of the data and observations that I
will share in the full presentation.

• The labs have a potential student FTE user base ranging
from 4800 to 34000. The size of the potential user base
seems to bear no relationship to the size of the collection.

• The labs agree on 9 purposes, though in varying
priority. Overall, the highest 2 priorities are a) to
promote integration of micro applications into the curriculum
and b) to provide resources for students in courses requiring
micros. One of the more intriguing purposes of 1 lab is to
enhance student and faculty recruitment.

• The software collections range in age from 5 years to 1
year. The number of titles, in order by collection age from
oldest to youngest:

663   300   150   300   75   46

• The dollars that each lab expects to spend for software
annually in the next 4 years range from 5000 to 15000.

• The respondents estimate that software discounts obtained by the labs range, on an average, from 30% to 75%.

• The number of pc's per campus ranges from 140 to 35. Lumping all the labs together, we're talking 21 microcomputer models. Three-quarters are IBM and Zenith, Macintosh, and Apple. Zenith edges out IBM. . . . There are 33 printer models.

• One lab is open an astonishing 114.5 hours a week--5 nights until 1:30 a.m., the other 2 nights until 11:30 p.m.

• In three labs, depending on the lab, either 1/3 or 1/2 or all of the pc's may be reserved in 2-hour blocks. All of the pc's in the other three labs are available on a first-come/first-served basis only. All labs impose a 1- or 2-hour limit on unreserved pc's if folks are waiting.

• All labs take precautions to preclude or discourage unauthorized copying of software. The most innovative precaution reported is the installation by 2 labs of anti-copying warnings on program disks.

• Three respondents believe their staffing is adequate and 3 believe their staffing is inadequate. The latter 3 indicated what staffing they thought would be adequate. . . . In terms of workstations in each lab, adequate staffing, either actual or fantasized, ranges from 4.6 workstations per FTE position to 21.75 workstations per FTE position.

• The biggest problems encountered by the campuses in establishing and maintaining these collections were/are software control, software maintenance, and user needs for assistance. Only 2 respondents confessed that their "biggest" problems remain unresolved.

• All of the respondents plan or hope to expand and upgrade their resources significantly within the next 4 years.

• These collections are at Texas A&M University, University of Wisconsin--Parkside, Texas Tech University, Florida Institute of Technology, Cornell University, and University of Michigan.

When I think of these collections and free-associate, I think like this: exciting, purposeful, popular, choices, hectic, friendly, expensive, fun, complicated, happy, the world is a better place because of them, true believers . . . Another way of putting it: I think of Christmas.

77

OPTICAL DIGITAL IMAGE STORAGE SYSTEM PROJECT

AT THE NATIONAL ARCHIVES AND RECORDS ADMINISTRATION

WILLIAM L. HOOTON, U.S. NATIONAL ARCHIVES

The National Archives is the official repository for the records of the Federal Government. With such an awesome task, automation must play a large role in its management. Digital image systems based on optical disk technology may provide some solutions to problems generated in this massive image storage and retrieval operation. These systems may offer significant benefits by enabling the Archives to rely on the use of electronic images instead of the original paper documents for research. This alone would provide important preservation advantages. Other potential advantages include the ease and speed of access of retrieval of the particular document requested. Even with these potential advantages, however, there are many unanswered questions regarding the suitability and applicability of such a system at the National Archives due to the particular nature of its holdings.

The National Archives is acquiring its own system to answer these questions about the applicability of this technology. This presentation will describe the major goals, considerations and strategies in system design and development. Our new contract with UNISYS Corporation will be discussed as will our plans for the future use of this technology.

NETWORKED MICROCOMPUTERS FOR
LIBRARY ADMINISTRATIVE COMPUTING NEEDS

Bonnie L. Hornbeck and Maureen Harden
University of California, San Diego

In 1983, the University of California, San Diego, Library committed $12,000 to the purchase of a 4-station microcomputer system that was to be devoted primarily to addressing the urgent word processing and data management needs that existed within the administrative units. One of the major criteria for the new system was that it be networked to allow for a multitasking, multiprocessing environment sharing peripherals. This was accomplished by purchasing a system with Z-80A microprocessor workstations running under a TurboDos operating system. Each workstation node had its own microprocessor with 64K RAM that was attached to a standard ASCII terminal. The processor-per-workstation along with multiple hard drives attached to the file server allowed multi-tasking and multi-processing while using single-user software.

It was anticipated that with the use of the new system, the Library's escalating campus-based word processing and typesetting costs would decline. Further, it was hoped that the Library would experience higher production and faster, more flexible data retrieval on a system independent of the campus owned and operated system. In addition, it was obvious that since the employees who were to use the system ranged from beginner to fairly sophisticated users, there was also an immediate need to provide training. To address training needs, standard off-the-shelf software (WordStar, dBase, and SuperCalc) was purchased in order to minimize training time. A user group was also formed during the initial stages of the system's use which enabled a small group of core users to become rapidly familiar with the network and with the variety of software provided for them. This resulted in a rapid increase in user sophistication that subsequently enabled the core group to produce a large base of trained users early in the start-up phase. As early as 10 months following the initial use of the system, Library Administration's networked system and training practices were providing a model for other campus departments and for other University of California campuses.

From 1983 to 1985, for an additional $13,000, the network grew to an 11-workstation, 13-user system. This system is capable of not only producing text using word processing, but also managing large personnel, salary, accounting, purchasing, and inventory files.

The menu-driven accounting and purchasing/receiving programs were developed by customizing programs in dBase II. Purchase orders can be printed from on-line input and reports produced that indicate the receiving status of an order or a particular item on the order. The accounting programs monitor and report expenditures for the total supplies, equipment, and other business activities of the library. The accounting module was carefully planned so that the most current transactions can be functionally manipulated and reported. SuperCalc is used for income accounting and other spreadsheet applications while equipment inventory is kept on "regular" dBase. Personnel management data bases and menu-driven dBase II programs were developed in-house to manage a myriad of functions relating to the personnel and salary administration of the Library's 600 employees. These include historical records on each employee; monitoring and analysis of all existing salary and staffing allocations; and "what if projections" for planning purposes. Additionally, the ability to extract and manipulate data from various files is used to create summary reports needed for cyclical university programs such as performance evaluation, merit increases and special service awards. Much of this work, performed manually in the past, is now done faster, with greater accuracy, and with greater flexibility in data management and retrieval.

The original 8-bit system is now being replaced by a larger, more sophisticated PC network using Advanced NOVELL network operating system with Ethernet cabling. Most of the programs developed and utilized on the smaller network are compatible with the 16-bit system. As expected the cost of some functions was reduced. Certain campus computer center costs dropped 69% from 1983/84 to 1985/86, a statistic solely attributable to the use of the microcomputer. Careful initial planning and a well-organized training program contributed to a successful administrative computing application.

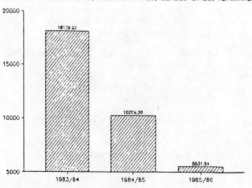

CAMPUS COMPUTER CENTER COSTS
FOR WORD PROCESSING, BIBLIOGRAPHIES, LEASED LINES, TERMINALS

MICROCOMPUTER KEYWORD INDEXING IN GOVERNMENT DOCUMENTS

Sheila E. Jaeger, University of Miami Library

Keyword indexes traditionally have acceptance in libraries as tools that provide subject access to substantial collections that are not otherwise fully subject cataloged. For government documents librarians the most notable example is the keyword index to the Monthly Catalog of U. S. Government Publications. In Florida, state documents have been keyword indexed by Florida Atlantic University since 1969. This index is published by the State Library of Florida and distributed through the state depository library program. Typically, as in the two examples given above, keyword indexing is done for large collections, using mainframe or mini-computers, almost always at a remote site. At the University of Miami Otto G. Richter Library we are experimenting with keyword indexing of well-exercised smaller collections using an IBM PC.

Primarily, KWICIE was written at the Richter Library to meet the need for a menu-driven program capable of generating simple keyword-in-context indexes of our Inter-governmental Organization (IGO) collections. To generate a KWIC index, the program, written in BASIC for an M300 IBM PC using PC DOS 2.0, manipulates three files. KWICIE automatically names these files, appropriately enough, Datafile, Keyword, and Stopword. When stored on a floppy disk, Datafile can handle up to 2250 of the abbreviated bibliographic records described below. Keyword, which is "built" automatically by KWICIE in the course of creating the index, and Stopword can share a second floppy. Input to Datafile and Stopword is accomplished by a few menu choices and responses to prompts. All of KWICIE's functions are simple enough that computer novices need only a short training session.

KWICIE's Datafile records have three fields, set to accept titles up to 115 characters long, holdings information up to 20 characters, and location symbols up to 23 characters. The title field is long enough to accomodate title cross references and in many cases is used to list additional subject terms. Since the entire title field is used for keyword extraction, these added subject terms will also be treated as keywords. KWICIE truncates all keywords at 20 characters as they are stored.

Our first index was generated in December 1985 using KWICIE Version 1.0. Working through a 2000 title Datafile, KWICIE took 7 hours to extract keywords, 168 hours to sort keywords and associated titles, and 6 hours to print a 500+ page index. The unacceptably long sort time was caused by a sort algorithm that required continuous reading and writing on the disks. The day after this first disk drive endurance test, work began on KWICIE Version 2.0.

KWICIE 2.0 extracts and sorts keywords in batch mode at the user's command, allowing the keyword index to be cumulated without having to repeat keyword extraction and sorting for an entire Datafile. As long as we use KWICIE with floppies and a 256K PC, we expect other functions to continue to be time consuming. The other serious limitation caused by the use of a PC, that of file size, has not yet been a problem for us in the projects we have chosen.

Our first project, which produced the index described above, covers our 15-20 IGO collections and includes significant monographs (1980-1985) and series titles with strong emphasis on statistical sources. We plan to produce annual supplements that will cumulate for four or five years, depending upon file size. Our second project integrates our varied and fragmented special location and reference collections into one keyword index. To staff members who work with these collections daily, their arrangement is logical and convenient. To substitute and new documents librarians, the keyword index sometimes offers the only simple route to a source.

We are offering a copy of KWICIE free to interested parties, with the understanding that the copyright is retained by the University of Miami Richter Library. Improvements in hardware (i.e. expansion boards, hard disks) will obviously shorten running times, but may require changes in the program. Modifying field sizes, adding or deleting fields, or even adding an optional field for additional subject terms cannot be done interactively. However, users with a knowledge of IBM BASIC should be able to modify the file format and the format of the printed indexes by revising the program.

MICROCOMPUTER LANS FOR USERS: USC'S OUTREACH SATELLITES

Lee David Jaffe, University of Southern California

This paper describes the installation of a local area network (LAN) in a library microcomputer user facility. It also presents considerations for other libraries contemplating a similar project.

The University of Southern California library is creating facilities -- called Satellites -- where faculty and students may use the latest information tools. While the Satellites center around a proposed mainframe network, currently their most prominent feature is the availability of microcomputers; between 18 and 24 work stations at each site. These are connected to the campus computing network, through which users have access to the library's online circulation system, a campus calendar and other services. Four stations also serve as InfoTrac terminals and another four are connected to Grolier's Electronic Encyclopedia. We also offer application and utility programs; a word processor, outline processor, PC-DOS, and disk utilities. We plan to add a data base management program soon and other software as we go.

Our design goal was one-stop-shopping, with many services available from any work station in the room. Our target audiences were novice and infrequent users. We sought a system that allowed combining different services at the terminal and ease of use and access. Managing circulation and security of software were additional concerns.

Our solution to these goals and concerns was installation of local area networks. LANs would manage software distribution, allow integration of services through a common interface, link each work station to the printer, and provide easy, menu-driven access to system features. We were also encouraged in this decision by the Library's past experience with a LAN: administration had been networked for more than a year. This also lead us to select the same network for our public installations.

The features of our system include the work stations, a file server, a printer, and connecting cables and adapter cards. Software in the server manages access to the system, files, and printer. Software in the work stations establishes the connection to the network. Menu software allows us to create custom screens with options to match the installed services.

Installation of the network proceeded in careful stages. A small network for testing by staff was followed by a trial system in a public area and later by a large-scale installation. Through this process we learned that 1) performance deteriorates

83

radically with use, 2) the system fails entirely at odd times, and 3) we could not connect as many stations as planned. The solution offerred by our vendor was a $20,000 hardware and software upgrade. At the time of writing we are trying to find an alternative solution. These limitations have forced us to make some adjustments.

On the up side, the Satellites are open to the public and the networks do offer greater capability than available with stand-alone systems. We have been able to integrate the online catalog, InfoTrac and Grolier's Encyclopedia, and offer a word processing program on a single terminal. Users have access with only a few key strokes and without having to swap a single disk. This is very close to the system which we set out to create.

The basic considerations in planning for and installing a LAN are whether a network offers realistic cost benefits over stand-alone configurations, whether networks offer service and capability advantages over the alternatives, and what steps users should take to ensure adequate functionality. For those libraries wishing to benefit from our experience, we can offer the following observations.

Local area networks vary greatly in features and cost. Hardware and software for our selected system, and many other systems, are expensive and priced on a per work station basis. It has been suggested that any stand-alone configuration will be cheaper than a network offerring equivalent capabilities. Cost is not a likely argument in favor of networking.

Instead there may be advantages of capability for which there are no alternatives at any cost. Though many of the features in our network might have been replicated using stand-alone microcomputers, they could not have been installed in the existing space. Additionally, our network provides a level of administrative control, a simple method of updating our services and a means of collecting statistics not available through any other configuration.

As to functionality, prevention is worth a ton of cure. The complexity of networks makes it difficult say how a system will perform in a particular situation. The risk is greater because costs are high and solutions may not be readily available. The only certainty comes with a reliable demonstration.

THE IN-HOUSE CONNECTION:
THE ONLINE SEARCHER AS DATABASE DESIGN EXPERT

Diane E.P. Johnson, Infodata Systems Inc.

Perhaps one of the clearest symbols of change in the librarian's online environment is that the phrase "online searching" no longer has a single, totally unambiguous meaning. Until about three years ago, in many institutions (other than airline ticket offices!) the most conspicuous consumers of interactive/online computer resources were reference librarians. Personnel and payroll offices might have been "computerized," or inventories computer-generated. But that data was probably managed by laboriously and mysteriously written special programs, devoid of documentation; worse, that data was often available only offline, with users forced to refer to print-outs whose retrieval criteria, formats, and even publication schedules were completely out of their control. In sharp contrast to this sad situation were online searchers, the priests and priestesses of an enlightened cult in which data formats were documented, retrieval flexible, and print formats more or less user-specified.

Now online access to many kinds of information, particularly consumer-related, is virtually pervasive. Does this mean that the glory days for online [bibliographic] searchers are past? Not necessarily; the days of the searchers' elite may be gone, but the knowledge we gained is still -- perhaps increasingly -- quite relevant. Many institutions are just beginning to automate control of management and business-related information and documents -- i.e., the usefulness (not to say necessity) of computers for managing internal data is being recognized; data bases of all kinds and sizes are being created in-house. And _here_ is where online searchers have the opportunity to offer their skills in the right place and at the right time: we can be of immense help in creating useful, useable, efficient databases.

We are familiar with almost all the parameters related to database design: we know data structures and how they affect retrieval, we know the value and drawbacks of controlled vocabularies and other indexing techniques, and we of course know how to do effective, efficient searches of many kinds; many of us even know how to train others in online searching. We know both national standards for data formats and de facto in-house styles, and can thus help impose some kind of "integrability" even in decentralized data processing environments. We are already familiar with users' information needs and usage patterns, and so start out with a good idea of their database needs. And finally, we may well have already mastered a database management system for our own library-related application, and hence have gained expertise that can be helpful to new database managers. Having recognized ourselves as most competent in the area of database design, the challenge, of course, is to advertise this capability within our institutions!

GOVDOX: A GOVERNMENT DOCUMENTS CHECK-IN SYSTEM

Chris Kiser and Clyde Grotophorst, George Mason University

As anyone who has ever maintained a collection of government documents can attest, it sometimes seems it takes more time to process a document than it did to produce in the first place. While no microcomputer system has yet succeeded in altering GPO requirements, systems such as GOVDOX can make processing much more efficient.

GOVDOX is a microcomputer-based check-in system, written in dBASE III and compiled via Nantucket's CLIPPER. It has been in use at George Mason University's Fenwick Library for three years--during which time we have made innumerable revisions to the system. Our initial effort used the CONDOR 3 database package, although to gain greater flexibility some months later we rewrote the system in dBASE II. The following year it was converted to dBASE III and early in 1986 completely rewritten to take advantage of Nantucket's CLIPPER compiler. In its latest form (Release 4.0), we have finally produced a product which meets both our original design goals: an easy-to-use system that is extremely fast. Compiling with CLIPPER has produced another benefit as well--we can now distribute the system to a wide audience since users do not need a copy of dBASE III to operate it.

Early versions of the system required the user enter many data elements for each document, but over time we have reduced the amount of information stored on each document to the following (field length in parentheses): SuDoc Number (30), Item Number (10), Title (74), Date (8), Subject (15), and Note (10). This streamlining of data entry is typical of most microcomputer applications--you usually discover that you do not need as much information as you first thought.

Features of the GOVDOX system include:

o SuDoc Number, Title, and Subject fields are indexed for fast retrieval
  (match found in less than 2 seconds in a database of 40,000+ records).
o During data entry, opeator may store information from the current
  record and import it to a new one. Very useful when successive
  entries differ only by one or two digits of a SuDoc number.
o Users may select to view and/or print all matching records.
o Matching records may also be written to a separate disk file.
o System reports elapsed time for all processing functions that
  take longer than a few seconds (this enables users to better
  schedule tasks like re-indexing, packing, etc).
o Editing function allows users to page forward and backward through
  the database to edit, delete, or 'un-delete' records.
o System maintains a separate database for deleted records. This
  provides an instantaneous report of records flagged for deletion.

o System sorts SuDoc numbers accurately (using SudoSort utility).
o System reports number of records in database and date of last
  update from main menu.
o Windows and 'bounce-bar' menus are used to simplify operation
  of the system.
o All prompts offer a default--to minimize keystrokes.
o Database is compatible with dBASE III/III+.

GOVDOX was initially designed to provide an online catalog for a
government documents collection--without much thought given to printing
the file. We later added the ability to generate a listing of all
documents but that ordering suffered from the same inaccuracy any user
of dBASE encounters when sorting SuDoc numbers. To solve this problem,
we have now developed a utility program (SudoSort) which can provide a
completely accurate SuDoc number sort of the database. The actual
algorithm used by SudoSort is fairly complex, but the process is
straightforward. SudoSort creates a copy of the GOVDOX database
inserting an additional field into each record. Working sequentially
through the database, SudoSort parses apart each SuDoc number, rebuilds
it in a form that dBASE can sort correctly, and copies this new
variation to the blank field. The database is sorted on the new field
then printed (the field created by SudoSort does not print).

If interested in obtaining a copy of the GOVDOX system, contact:

Systems Librarian, Library Systems Office
Fenwick Library, George Mason University
4400 University Drive, Fairfax, VA 22068
(703) 323-2317

System Requirements:

IBM-PC or any other MS-DOS machine
256K RAM memory

Storage Requirements:

Version 4.0 (with Subject/Note fields)   20,000 records = 5.4 Mb
Version 3.2 (w/o Subject or Note fields) 20,000 records = 4.5 Mb

Library Image and Graphic Based Technology Launches Forward!

Executive Summary for SCIL 1987
by
Norman Kline

The recent surge in interest and development of desktop publications and desktop communications hardware and software has brought forward several powerful solutions in storing and retrieving digitized information.

These advances include systems that allow the storage of large amounts of information to a hard-disk or optical media and then its retrieval by a set of networked users. Some systems are built as generic information filing or database packages, while fewer are tailored specifically for the Library market.

Hardware:

The leading edge computer for cost-effective Image and Graphic systems is the Macintosh family of micros.

The Macintosh family offers a full line of workstations which can easily and inexpensively be networked for a small group of workers through AppleTalk or one or more building thousands of miles apart using Ethernet cabling.

File servers and disk servers, including CDROM and WORM, are available. The communication and graphic standards built into the Macintosh technology are followed by all Macintosh developers. These standards allow easy transfer of data from one application to another.

Software:

Several unique solutions have been built using Apple's technology and third party's expertise.

FileVision:

This file system offers a unique capability for storing images and data retrieving them using the graphics interface to the utmost.

MacCards:

MacCards takes advantage of the graphic user interface of the Macintosh to provide an very friendly, easy to learn yet powerful system for producing library cards and labels.

The Mac Library System:

This package is a multi-user, multi-functional library system which again uses the Macintosh User Interface to effectively automate an intensive text operation.

DigiBase:

The DigiBase document library provides a system for scanning large numbers of documents into an indexed central server. Multiple scanning stations can be setup scanning documents while multiple user stations can browse and retrieve documents to be printed on laser or high quality dot matrix printers.

Conclusions:

The continued maturity of standards and use of intuitive object oriented user interfaces will increase the power of library systems while making them easier to learn and use.

SAFEGUARDING YOUR MICRO DATABASE: BACKUP OPTIONS

Stephen L. Koss, Mobius Management Systems, Inc.

An interesting and little-noticed outgrowth in the increased use of microcomputers is the shift in responsibilities for system operations. In the days of mainframes and minis only, such system administrative tasks as equipment maintenance, supplies ordering, capacity management, electrical load planning, disaster planning, database backup, and security were largely transparent to end users. These tasks were almost entirely the domain of the data processing department.

Of all these areas which must usually now be assumed by the microcomputer user, the most significant is database backup. Before automation, database backup was not a serious issue - you could only lose your "database" if you lost all of your paper records in a fire or comparable disaster. If you were on a mainframe, the data center took care of backup planning and off-site storage. Now, with microcomputer systems, you can lose your database as easily as a bent diskette, a failed hard disk drive, or the improbably simple "C> format" command.

Definitions

Before tackling the issue of database backups, three definitions are needed:

> File backup - The process by which secondary copies of data files, programs, and software packages are created, updated, and stored.

> File restore - The process by which backup files are used to replace corrupted or lost files.

> Forward recovery - The process by which data added to the damaged file after the last backup but before it was corrupted, is reentered to the system. In other words, how do you get back to where you were?

Backup Principles

There are myriad details and concerns associated with the frequency, timing, and procedures of backup. However, the fundamentals of database backup can be summed up in six basic rules of thumb.

> Thumb Rule #1 - Back up any data files or programs whose loss would be a hardship or worse. A good hypothetical question to ask is whether the removal by theft of any files would result in replacement problems.

> Thumb Rule #2 - Frequency of backup of your individual files and programs is a function of the value of the data, its transience (rate of change), level of effort to complete forward recovery, and feasibility of forward recovery.

90

Thumb Rule #3 - One backup is not enough for active recordkeeping or operational system files such as circulation. There must be a policy of rotating periodic backups and regular checking of backup media.

Thumb Rule #4 - Do not keep all of your backups on-site for critical files. A rotating off-site backup of crucial files should be maintained.

Thumb Rule #5 - Make backup policy firm but flexible, and easy to implement. Assign backup responsibilities explicitly, create a schedule of backup activities, and make sure it is followed. Use batch files or other software tools to make backup as quick and easy as possible.

Thumb Rule #6 - Don't stand pat. Continuous review of new applications, new data files, and new backup technology options is necessary.

Backup Tools and Techniques

Just as the number of microcomputer-based software tools has expanded continuously in the last few years, so has the number of approaches to file backup. As is so often the case with so many choices, there is no universal right answer. The right technology for a given microcomputer environment is critically dependent on the applications involved and their size and usage. The best approach for individual microcomputers doing independent word processing is not likely to be the best approach for a multi-user local area network.

The range of choices is almost staggering, and it is still growing. At the low end is diskette-based backup, using the DOS Copy or Backup commands, or a third party backup program (such as Fastback or TakeTwo). Removable cartridge systems such as the Bernoulli Box provide an approach with greater capacity.

At a still greater level of cost and capability are so-called streaming tape devices. Currently, users can select from 1/4-inch tape units (the most common), 1/2-inch tape cartridges, 9-track tape drives, and even videocassette tapes. Optical disks are also available for permanent (unchangeable) archiving. Another approach involves continuous backup to a hard disk as you update your data files.

Finally, two other sophisticated approaches involve the use of minicomputers or mainframes, if you have access to them. One approach uses bulk file transfers to virtual DOS disk files on a mainframe disk, based on micro-mainframe link products. The other uses software such as IBM's PC Support product to place PC files on a minicomputer-based virtual disk file, either for periodic transfer or for real-time interaction. These products complete the circle to some extent, returning the responsibility for backups and backup rotation to the data center.

91

DEVELOPING THE PROGRAM IN-HOUSE:

PLANNING, PROCEDURE, DESIGN

Lynda S. Kuntz, Consultant, Potomac Consultants

Can a small technical library staff develop library system requirements to support the parent organization; analyze state-of-the-art commercial systems; and having determined that commercial packages are too costly and incompatible with the library requirements, design and develop a unique integrated library system utilizing dBASE III, Wordstar and PC-Talk? The answer is YES if the library is in the U.S. Army Concepts Analysis Agency (CAA), Bethesda, Maryland. How we accomplished these tasks is the essence of my presentation.

The mission of the library is to provide reference and in-depth research to the Agency. CAA's mission is to perform studies and analyses of military logistics and manpower planning. The library's staff consists of two librarians, a library technician and a security specialist. Its annual budget for acquisitions, online services, supplies and equipment at the time of automation was $50,000. Its collection consists of approximately 2500 books, 13000 documents and 200 serial titles.

Defining the systems requirements is crucial to a fair and complete evaluation of commercial systems and is invaluable in designing an in-house system. In the systems requirements stage, we found that the one item which distinguishes this library, is its need to merge Online Computer Library Center (OCLC) machine readable cataloging (MARC) records with non-MARC records. Cataloging information for books and serials comes from OCLC while the bibliographic information for most documents is from Defense Technical Information Center (DTIC).

An evaluation of one commercial system (Sydney) against the requirements list illustrates the comparison process. While the evaluation of commercial systems was ongoing, the possibility of developing a system in-house was pursued. In-house development was attractive from the aspect of specializing the system to meet unique needs. Development in-house required taking the systems requirements list and locating or writing programs which accomplished these tasks. The resources for writing an integrated system from scratch was not available. Rather the in-house development focus was on locating programs that accomplish library tasks and then combining them into one system.

The design process of the in-house integrated library system using dBASE III, Wordstar and PC-TALK included decisions on data elements, on menu options, and on the

order of automation.   Data elements include those that are
searchable   or are necessary for identification of the item.
The menus offer the end user search by author, title,
subject,   series,   originating source or report number.
Searching includes Boolean logic in the title and subject
fields and between the author and title fields. The order of
automation was online catalog, acquisitions and cataloging
functions and circulation and serials control.

     In the small specialized library environment, an in-
house developed ILS can be justified based on cost factors
and the need to accommodate special materials.   In addition
this approach provides to the library staff the opportunity
to learn how to use microcomputer technology to accomplish
repetitive library tasks.

SELECTING SOFTWARE: PRINCIPLES AND PRACTICES
James LaRue, Lincoln Library

1 What do you want to do?

   1.1 Make list of desired tasks and features

      1.1.1 Pie-in-the-sky

      1.1.2 But be specific

      1.1.3 Invite staff participation

   1.2 Put list in order of importance

      1.2.1 Mark what's dispensable -- and what isn't

   1.3 Begin trying to match list

2 Do you _really_ need an automated solution?

3 Two kinds of software

   3.1 Educational

   3.2 Applications or "productivity"

4 Concerns

   4.1 Choose the software first -- if possible

   4.2 Which computer(s)?

      4.2.1 Memory and storage requirements

      4.2.2 Other hardware requirements

         Peripheral devices (printer, special monitor, modem, etc.)

         Special function boards (color-graphics, clock card, etc.)

      4.2.3 Computing environment

     Other computers used and the need for some compatibility

     Hardware (direct or through network) or file

DOWNLOADING, REFORMATTING, AND ADDING HOLDINGS INFORMATION
TO MEDLINE SEARCH RESULTS

Peter M. LePoer, The Ohio State University Health Sciences Library

1. GOALS

Goals of this project were: 1) to provide better-looking, more easily
understandable search results for patrons by eliminating extraneous material,
and providing citations in a uniform format for results from different
databases with consistent and clear labels for the different parts of a
record; 2) to include some type of holdings information in the print-out, thus
eliminating look-up steps and fruitless trips to the stacks by patrons for
journals not received.

2. METHODS

In order to match downloaded citations against the library's serial holdings,
it was necessary to have an up-to-date serials database which included a field
in common with the downloaded citations. Because of the vagaries and possible
duplication of journal titles, the National Libarary of Medicine Unique
Journal Code, a three character alphanumeric code for each of the journals
indexed by NLM, was chosen as the element on which to match citations and
holdings. A serials holding list maintained on the campus mainframe was
downloaded to a PC, put into a STAR database, and the journal codes added to
the records.

Search results are downloaded using QMODEM, a "shareware" general purpose
telecommunications package. Extraneous material is removed from the resulting
file of citations. Records are then imported into a STAR database, matched
against the serial holdings database, and holdings statements from the records
that match are added to the citations. The resulting bibliography is then
printed, with either the titles which are held by the library marked, or
actual holdings information added to the printed citations. The citations are
sorted by journal to further facilitate shelf look-up.

3. SOFTWARE

A compiled BASIC program was written which removes search statements, record
numbers, and system prompts by checking the beginning of each line for field
tags & other clues (depending on the database). It deletes the line if it is
not a part of a record, makes small format changes and creates a new file
under a different name with the cleaned-up citations.

STAR (a database management system for handling large text-oriented databases)
was chosen for various reasons. The most important feature for our purposes
was a file import facility used to add search results to a database - STAR
supports a format which allows direct import of most bibliographic database
records with very little modification. The other important feature is a
cross-database update facility which performs the match on journal code and
adds holdings information to search records. The software also supports a
macro capability which automates the process by condensing all the steps into
a few two-key commands. All of these features are accessible without
programming, thus speeding up development time.

4. IMPLEMENTATION

Searching and downloading is done by the reference librarians who take the search requests while on the reference desk. The librarians have been using QMODEM on the PC for several months. The software provides an easily-learned procedure for downloading results. The librarians store results for each search in a separate file.

Further processing is then done by staff and students. Necessary background tasks include maintaining the serials list, and adding new codes for journals added by NLM.

REMOTE SEARCHING AN ON-LINE CATALOG USING A CHECKOUTABLE MICROCOMPUTER: A SERVICE FOR FACULTY AT A UNIVERSITY CAMPUS

Michael W. Loder, Pennsylvania State University/Schuylkill Campus

The Schuylkill Campus is one of seventeen "Commonwealth campuses" in the Pennsylvania State University system. It has an enrollment of approximately seven hundred students, most with freshman and sophomore status. Thirty-five full-time faculty plus a few part-time instructors offer these students, and other area residents, a complete range of lower division courses. These faculty enjoy the same status as their associates at the main campus at University Park and are under similar pressures to conduct and publish research. Demand for research service is small but concentrated—most of the faculty must rely on the University library system for at least initial research needs.

Although the campus library maintains an adequate collection for the lower-division course offerings of the campus, it is not a research library. Serious researchers must rely on phone links and LIAS (Library Information Access System), Penn State's own online catalog system, to gain access to the main collections at University Park and the collections at other Common-wealth campuses.

In February, 1984, LIAS became fully available at the Schuylkill Campus. Along with terminals located in the library, we received a local phone line allowing persons with terminals or micros and modems to remote-dial-access LIAS. While there were no restrictions regarding public access to this local line, it was primarily intended as a remote access point for the campus community. The number was local, log-on procedures were minimal and there was no charge.

We felt that this ability to search the catalog from any location could be one of LIAS's strongest features. Yet few of the local faculty had either terminals or microcomputers and therefore few could take advantage of this service.

In order to allow more of the faculty to remote search LIAS, in 1984, with support from a University Faculty Scholarship Support Fund (FSSF) grant, we purchased an Apple IIc with carrying case, monitor, modem and printer. The Apple IIc was chosen because of its transportability and because at that time virtually all the micros on campus were Apple II's. In January, 1985 we began offering this package, together with the AppleTerm software, to the faculty and staff on an as-needed basis.

We publicized this new service with flyers, announcements and a live

98

demonstration. Despite these efforts the faculty showed little interest in using the micro for remote searching even though the setup worked and worked well. The microcomputer did see steady faculty use but mainly for word-processing.

At the end of the first year of offering this service, we had had twenty checkouts involving eight different instructors. One fourth of the faculty had used the machine, but on only three occasions had the machine been used for its original purpose of remote searching LIAS.

Viewed from the point-of-view of our original, narrow purpose, the service was a failure. Yet the machine was and is being used, and being used heavily, and there was an unexpected benefit of the program, and for that reason, I would recommend such a project to others.

Offering a special service to the faculty stimulated use of other services, some of which had previously been offered, but not used, others which we were inspired to offer due to the acceptance of the checkoutable micro. We started encouraging the use of the library's Macintosh personal computer for the creation of instructional graphics and small item word-processing such as syllabi production and tests. Over on hundred faculty and staff uses have been recorded on this machine in the library since October, 1985. A correcting typewriter set aside for faculty use has been in use virtually every day. Audio-visual services use in general has increased. Some of that use can be related to the publicity concerning Remote-Use.

We began to see these non-print activities as something that could be rolled under one heading, "Library Special Services for Faculty," and instead of one project we had a program—a program that we are still adding to and building. Offering one special service turned out to be the key to identifying faculty needs and interests in terms of services we could offer. It also got the library into the "computer business" in an easy, inexpensive way and produced goodwill.

While dial-up access to LIAS was of little interest to the faculty, it has been popular with the community at large, particularly the area high schools, the local Intermediate Unit and the district public library. Its availability has resulted in interlibrary loan requests from those libraries. We use Remote LIAS for demonstrations and for searching LIAS when all the library terminals are in use. As a "Service to the public" it is worth a great deal because we can promote LIAS as a catalog available to all, not just the campus community. So dial-up LIAS is serving a public, if a different one than originally intended.

END

99

LINKING OPTICAL STORAGE DEVICES
AND
LOCAL AREA NETWORKS

John B. Lowe
Principal Programmer
U.C. Division of Library Automation

Two emerging and converging technologies have the potential to
revolutionize the way we communicate with each other and how we
remember what we communicate. Optical disk devices make it possible
to organize and retain almost limitless amounts of information more
economically and conveniently than ever before. Developments in
networking make it possible to share with others what we've retained
and organized.

Some of the most cherished dreams of the electronic scholarship may
be implemented through these technologies: the paperless office,
unlimited and instant access to the accumulated store of Man's
knowledge, and so on.

However, after giving these lofty notions a few nods, we must now
roll up our sleeves and put our shoulders to the wheel and make it
happen.

What are the easy parts of this endeavor? What are the hard
parts? Where is there room to spare, and where will the
bottlenecks appear?

This paper discusses an attempt to create a system to realize some
of these dreams. Our efforts encompass the use of broadband local
area network facilities, existing 5.25" and 12" WORM optical disks,
the TCP/IP telecommunications protocol, and IBM PC/AT
microcomputers acting in concert to provide distributed access to a
variety of types of information.

FROM MANUAL TO AUTOMATED: FIRST HAND LESSONS FROM NLS READS

Jane Mandelbaum, National Library Service For The
Blind And Physically Handicapped, LOC
Lorri Kosterich, Mobius Management Systems, Inc.

Moving a library's operations from a manual system to an automated one
is a very complicated and arduous undertaking. However burdensome the
conversion may be, automation almost always reaps a good payback for the
effort, including increased productivity and reliable statistics and
information. Thorough planning is of the utmost importance and is the key
to a successful automation conversion effort. Even with good planning,
the automation conversion effort can be a nervewracking nightmare; without
it, the automation conversion effort can easily be a disaster.

There are many preparatory and concurrent tasks an automator should
perform, conducive to a smooth transition. We have divided these tasks
into six planning areas, defined below. (Although we have included "Needs
Analysis" as the first planning area, our talk will assume that automation
has already been justified and the hardware and software selected.)

Needs Analysis

-- Does the library really need to automate? - What functions?
-- Cost/benefit analysis (feasibility)
-- Specification of functional requirements and hardware needs
-- Hardware/software selection
-- Staffing requirements
-- Budget approval

Pre-Automation Planning

-- Speak to or visit other users of system about their start-up
-- Finalize equipment requirements
-- Finalize funding needs
-- Prepare floor plans for equipment and electrical wiring
-- Decide on any changes to be made from manual to automated
   system
-- Evaluate file conversion alternatives and approaches

Staff

-- Involvement and participation
-- Training and hand holding
-- Staffing regular daily work during automation effort
-- Assigning system management responsibilities

101

Support Services

-- Hardware installation
-- Software installation and training
-- Technical support
-- Equipment maintenance

Organizing the Conversion Effort

-- Clean up the old files
-- Assign values to new data elements in advance if possible
-- Decide which data items are to be entered (consider limits such as age of data and storage capacity)
-- Choose feasible conversion scheme - (consider parallel testing, service level to patrons, closing off portions of collection for conversion, graduated roll-out)
-- Prioritize data element input based on modules to be implemented first
-- Conversion staffing (volunteers, key operators, library staff)
-- Time requirements - use Gantt charts or Critical Path charts

Installation and Post-Installation

-- Hardware and software acceptance testing
-- Quality control during start-up
-- Production cutover
-- Beware the informal system
-- Supplemenatary staff training needs

While automating twelve Libraries for the Blind and Physically Handicapped with a multi-user, micro-based circulation system, READS (Reader Enrollment And Delivery System), we have observed several key characteristics which seem to differentiate successful automation conversions from those who experienced more difficulty or hardship. Chief among these characteristics are the following:

-- Qualifications of system manager (adaptability, attention to detail, learns quickly, and minimal computerphobia)
-- Preparedness of staff (computer preparedness, application preparedness, and psychological commitment)
-- Local technical assistance
-- Adequate funds to meet contingencies
-- Organization of the effort
-- Open-mindedness (figure out how to make the system work for you)
-- Level of effort and time committed

102

DEVELOPING A CORPORATE LIBRARY CIRCULATION SYSTEM USING DBASE III

Nancy J. Mandeville, General Foods Corp.

At General Foods, a menu-driven circulation system was developed in dBase III for the Technical Center Library. This system allows the library staff to search and access circulation records by a variety of fields, including accession number and title. Also, overdue notices and various reports are produced. Our records are more up-to-date and accurate, and we are circulating more books than before.

HARDWARE AND SOFTWARE

This system runs on an IBM-PC (256K memory, DOS 3.1) with a Mountain DriveCard 10-megabyte internal hard disk. We use an Epson FX-185 printer. The software is dBASE III from Ashton-Tate which is a relational database management system. We also use an add-on program called Quickindex from Fox and Geller.

LIBRARY ENVIRONMENT

This is a research library with about 3,000 books in circulation. The system tracks both library and desk copy books. The previous manual system, requiring two sets of cards, was difficult to keep up-to-date. We also had no way to do overdues efficiently which resulted in a large book loss. These were the main reasons for automating the files. The library staff specified the system, and the code was written by a programmer in our Computer Applications group. This system was designed as an interim system to serve for about two years until we get an online catalog.

SYSTEM DESCRIPTION

The system is menu-driven, which required twenty-five pages of dBase code. There are four items on the main menu:

1. Check out / Return / Edit
2. Search the database
3. Print reports
4. Pack and re-index the database

Each of these is broken down into sub-menus. The database can be searched by accession number, call number, record number, title, and author.

Reports can be printed sorted by author, title, or call
number. The system determines which books are overdue
based on the due date entered when the book is checked
out. We print and distribute overdue notices weekly.
First and second notices are generated. We can change the
type of record from library to desk copy by editing a
field. A report which lists all books assigned to a
borrower can also be printed. This is very useful
when people transfer or leave the company.

It took six months to get the system up and running. That
included the initial specification, writing the code,
debugging and rewriting, writing the manual, entering the
data and training the staff. This was about twice our
initial optimistic estimate of three months.

STAFF TRAINING

This was one of the first microcomputer systems the staff
used, so we had to do quite a bit of training. The
hardest part for them to learn was the hard disk, mainly
using the directory and backing up the files. They really
had no trouble using the menu-driven dBase program. We
had to emphasize consistency in data entry so that
authors' names went in last name first, and initial
articles such as "the" were not entered. It also took a
few months before they could recover from errors on their
own.

ADVANTAGES AND DISADVANTAGES

The main advantage of the system is that we can type the
information in only once and sort it many ways such as by
title and borrower. Our records are now more accurate and
up-to-date. We can also produce overdue reports which are
very effective in reducing book loss. Disadvantages
include indexing time which initially took one hour. We
then added Quickindex which cut the time down to fifteen
minutes. Since the system is on a microcomputer, it can
only be accessed by one person at a time.

RECOMMENDATIONS

It was relatively easy to create the database and define
the fields after a one-day training session in dBase.
However, designing sophisticated menu-driven sytems
requires quite a bit more training. I recommend working
with someone who has programming experience if possible,
or taking an advanced course in dBase before starting a
major system.

104

AN OVERVIEW OF THE IN-HOUSE ILS PROJECT
IN A SMALL TECHNICAL LIBRARY

Margaret Martinez, DALIS Automated Systems

If you believe its time to consider the possibilities of
automation in your own library, be aware of several important
realities before considering an in-house integrated library
system(ILS). The greatest challenge is that an in-house project
is time-consuming and exhaustive work. It certainly sounds much
easier to buy and implement an off-the-shelf software package
which has already been tested and proven capable.

So why would you even consider an in-house ILS project given
the availability of today's sophisticated technology? This
paper proposes some reasons why a small technical library might
consider such a project with special emphasis placed on the
staff's role in the development of an in-house system. The most
important questions discussed are:

--What makes the in-house ILS a profitable and satisfying
  experience?
--What should be considered before beginning an in-house ILS
  project?
--What are the economics of an in-house ILS and what
  resources are required?
--When don't you want to consider an in-house ILS?
--What is the future of an in-house ILS?
--How does an in-house project affect the concept of
  standardization?
--And finally, what are the advantages of an in-house ILS
  over an off-the-shelf software package?

Several conclusions are drawn which might be useful to
other professionals posing the same questions. Whether we
actually automate or not, we must deal with these and similiar
questions to stay abreast of the rapid changes in our
profession.

EVALUATING THE POTENTIAL OF OPTICAL TECHNOLOGY AND ITS
INTERACTION WITH TRADITIONAL DATA DELIVERY MEDIA

Karen S. McConnell, Gulf States Utilities Co.

EXECUTIVE SUMMARY:

The increasing interest in optical disks has prompted
the creation of new products of interest to libraries.
Continuing increases in the popularity of this medium will
lead to a realization of information available at low cost
for everyone. The problems will be finding new ways to
access the information more effectively. However, the
promises for this technology discussed in the literature of
library and information technology are finally beginning to
unfold. The development of this mass storage and
distribution medium as a tool for more effective information
access should cause librarians to study how this technology
can be applied to their needs.

Many of the "new" CD-ROM products are virtually the same
as existing microform products, but provided in the optical
disk medium. The benefits of such systems have been touted
as cheap searching, unlimited use, fixed costs, and so on.
Realistically, most of these products provide access for one
user, on one machine, with no remote updating capabilities.
The online databases, however, can be updated as frequently
as necessary, and will continue to be used for current data.

While the optical technology may never replace online
databases, other applications using these disks will enable
libraries and other information providers to maintain,
retrieve, and deliver digitized data in an effective manner.
Several systems are already providing basic services on
laser disk, with telecommunication interface to the online
database for more current or more extensive data. This data
can consist of library holdings and/or records, company
financial and operating information, private databases, or
even video images. The use of "jukeboxes" even further
expands the quantity of data the systems can access.

Information providers should begin thinking in terms of
a system that will combine resource sharing and their
integrated library system functions. The large, expensive
systems now required to run integrated library software to
meet the requirements of efficient storage of the large
database, and quick response to demands of multiple users,
are soon to be outmoded. Optical storage devices could be
assigned the task of handling inquiries to the full MARC
format database, and then verifying the location of material

in a regional union list. Take this idea a step further, and the catalog users could even access the availability information for each location. Searches for the material would not then tie up communications lines, and dial-up access could handle updates to the central system as well as interlibrary loans.

This system does not now exist, but it is possible. The optical storage technology is emerging; the microprocessor evolution is continuing; local area networks exist now; large capacity hard disk drives are becoming less expensive; and telecommunications are getting faster. The obstacles at this point include: no software to do the job, immature optical disk market, vested interest in existing large systems, and reluctance to commit to new technology while components continue to evolve. It will be up to the information providers to communicate that the need for this type of system is sufficient to indicate financial success for a product.

An existing system, HAYSTACK II from Information Marketing International, not actually being marketed to libraries, is a model for use in applying this technology to library requirements. This system was designed for use by the military and defense contractors to increase productivity and reduce costs in all areas dealing with the military hardware and spare parts life cycle. This system is used by supply, logistics, purchasing, engineering, or any other group needing to search and retrieve parts information quickly and easily. Because originally marketed as an online database, HAYSTACK resembles many of those used daily by libraries.

The real benefit of optical technology to information providers and receivers is not having more data inless space or for less money, because the information itself does not even become more relevant or useful. The benefit is having more valuable information available for users, and the ability to justify the increased consumption of that information. As evidenced by leading edge technologies of the past, the new will not replace the old, but rather will be enhanced by it. Libraries need to be ready and knowledgeable about their effective use, and to provide the incentive for the producers to design the products. Large users will invest in the technology initially, but grass roots information providers will finally create the innovative applications. Is that not the way libraries have managed to lead in prior information technology breakthroughs?

107

AI and Expert Systems: the State of the Art

David R. McDonald, University of Michigan Library

Expert systems are computer programs that use human like
traits, such as logic, to assist in solving problems. Such
systems are begininng to emerge from the laboratory and make
their way into manufacturing, office, and educational settings.
This paper describes differences between expert system and
other types of computing, briefly touches on the history of
expert system development, identifies different system
and describes some of the projects that are working on expert
systems in the library and information retrieval fields.

Expert systems differ from traditional data processing and
from other areas of artificial intelligence (AI) in a number of
ways. First expert systems focus on knowledge, symbolic
representation, symbolic inference, and heuritic search.
Second, expert systems focus on specific problem solving
strategies, rather than on the more general "weak methods" of
AI. And finally, expert system use self-knowledge generated
during the execution of the program.

Work on expert systems began in the early 1970's with
several systems emerging by the mid-1970's. Early systems
focused on relatively narrow topics in medicine, chemistry,
geology, and mathematics. Stanford, MIT, and Carnegie-Mellon
were the centers of activity.

Expert systems typically fall into one of three
"architectures": (1) rule-based, (2) frame-based, or (3) a
combination of the two. Rule-based systems are best suited
to well defined, stand-alone problems. Frame-based systems
are better suited to more ambiguous, interrelated probems.

Expert systems are typically used to interpret, predict,
diagnose, design, plan, monitor, debugg, repair, instruct, or
control. Interest in expert systems within libraries and
information retrieval is quickly building. Researchers at
Western Illinois University are working to develop a system
that will help dtermine what cataloging rules to use in
descriptive cataloging. At SUNY/Buffalo work is in progress to
develop an experty system to provide reference service for
government documents.

That expert systems have a place in libraries and information retireval is clear. How successful such system will be in meeting users' needs will be limited only by our imagination.

Online Industry High School Programs

Mary G. McMahon, BRS Information Technologies

BRS Information Technologies has maintained an active
committment to the educational community since 1977 when
BRS received a grant from the National Institute of Education to computerize the NIE file of information on promising
practices. In keeping with this ongoing tradition, BRS
offers a range of educational services which are continually
updated and enhanced.

The hundreds of high schools currently online with
BRS subscribe to BRS/Educator, BRS/Instructor, or both. BRS/
Educator is an educational rate subscription plan used by
professionals in the K-12 educational community who are
searching for research rather than instructional purposes.
Searches performed for school administrators, for teachers or
principals, are performed with BRS/Educator passwords.

BRS/Instructor is the discounted, instructional program,
used whenever actual instruction on online searching is taking
place. Instructor passwords are used when a librarian does an
initial demonstration for a large group of students, when
students do practice searches in small teams, when an individual student initially goes solo, all of these situations
describe sound instructional applications. Over the past
several years we have seen an incredible upsurge of interest
in teaching students how to search.

For years, BRS had provided an instructional program
called the Library School Program that was available only to
instructors of online searching at Schools of Library or
Information Science. During the early eighties BRS received
a steadily increasing stream of inquiries from teachers in
settings other than library schools who were either already
teaching online searching or who wanted to teach online
searching. In answer to this demand, in mid-1985 BRS
announced an updated, more flexible instructional service
called BRS/Instructor, available to any instructor of a
formal, structured program teaching online searching.

The response has been quite enthusiastic. The number of
instructional passwords increased from appxoximately 300 to
well over 1500 during the first six months of availability.
BRS/Instructor subscribers now include indivivduals spanning a
wide range of academic levels, from sixth grade teachers
through professors in graduate programs. The curricular
applications in the elementary and secondary schools vary
widely. Some schools are centering the instruction on the
acquisition of library skills, on the awareness of information
science. Others use the instruction of online searching as a
supplement to a course in a specific discipline area, such as

110

Chemistry, Psychology, Current Events, or Computer Science. Still others have incorporated teaching online searching as a component of a logical thinking skills curriculum.

The Pennsylvania Department of School Library Media Services administers the LIN-TEL Project (Linking Information Needs - Technology, Education and Libraries). Through LIN-TEL, over one hundred educational sites throughout Pennsylvania access BRS with a combination of Educator and Instructor passwords. Most member sites are high school libraries. A few universities, middle and elementary schools, are also included. The network's size allows for unusually well-coordinated support services. New members can confer with experienced colleagues. Network business, such as meeting announcements, and inter-library loan, is conducted through MSGS, a message switching service on BRS. A student search-off contest is held each spring. A committee of LIN-TEL members developed a curriculum guide on online searching for use primarily at the high school level.

Another area where educators are active online is the state of Washington. A series of handbooks produced in Olympia describe online applications in the schools. Program specialists provide ongoing training and support to library media specialists and teachers.

With both BRS/Instructor and BRS/Educator, the searcher has a choice of menus or commands. Both offer the latest, state-of-the-art software capabilities. BRS will continue to enhance the educational services to maintain the highest quality of information retrieval.

References

Kachel, D. E. (1986). "Online Bibliographic Searching: A Pilot Project". School Library Journal, 32, 28-31.
Motamatsu, N. R., & Newman, J. A. (1986) Research Goes To School III - Going Online With Students. Olympia, WA: Published uder Chapter 2 - ECIA.
State Library of Pennsylvania (1985). Pennsylvania Online: A Curriculum Guide For School Library Media Centers. Harrisburg, PA: Pennsylvania Department of Education.

WORKSTATION ERGONOMICS AND ENVIRONMENT

R Bruce Miller, Indiana University Libraries

Ergonomics is the study of how people relate to their
environment. The focus in this presentation is on the
physical parameters in workstation design for visual
display terminal (VDT) and microcomputer use in libraries.
Guidelines are given that can be applied in a variety of
situations, including: public sites, circulation, OPAC,
reference, and technical services/administration.

Equipment design features are outlined to provide
background for selection decisions. Furniture and seating
design issues are discussed. Illumination and glare
factors are explained. Guidelines and reasons for rest
periods and eye care are given. A brief annotated
bibliography will be distributed.

Basic workstation dimensions

Note: Use of a tiltable monitor with good
glare/reflection control allows these guidelines
to be modified so that the top of the screen is
below eye level.

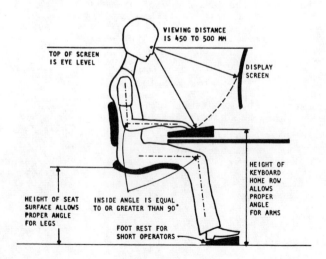

SOFTWARE FOR LIBRARY APPLICATIONS

Todd Miller, Information Access Company

Software developers must keep in mind the ultimate users of their product. For software directed toward reference applications in a library, two groups of people are kept in mind: the busy reference librarian who will have little or no time for training and the patron who may have no knowledge of computers or complex online search protocol.

The software developers goal must be to deliver the perfect package--one that offers all desirable features with ease of use; however, the realist knows that this objective is not often attainable. Therefore, a software package for use by non-technical people must be structured to allow for easy enhancement to respond to changing needs and the realities of use.

Software developers are dealing with a volatile hardware market that can make today's innovations obsolete tomorrow. As much as possible, they must make their package hardware independent, so that it can be easily ported to new systems or support new peripherals as they become available.

Software programs for use in libraries must have self-diagnostics to identify problems so that non-technical users can isolate hardware faults from software glitches. Built in diagnostics programming is often the most challenging area of hardware development.

Search protocol for reference software must consider the skills of the eventual user as well as the responsiveness of the storage media used.

PROVIDING SUBJECT ACCESS TO MICROCOMPUTER SOFTWARE

Joan S. Mitchell, Carnegie Mellon University

Microcomputer software poses special access problems for both catalog users and the cataloger. Access is needed not only to the author, title, and subject of the software, but to other aspects such as the system requirements. Some of this information is accessible from the descriptive cataloging; some must be provided through the subject headings and classification. This paper describes user access needs and how records can be developed to best meet those needs.

Users looking for software need access to some or all of the following: title, author, producer, programming language, operating system, machine and system requirements, age level or degree of difficulty, and genre or subject of software. It is necessary that access be developed to all these areas. It is not necessary, however, for the subject headings to be the sole source of this access. In evaluating access to software one must look at the descriptive cataloging, the subject headings, the classification, and the capabilities of the catalog in which such records are stored and retrieved.

Descriptive Cataloging
The basic source for the descriptive cataloging of microcomputer software is *Guidelines for Using AACR2 Chapter 9 for Cataloging Microcomputer Software*. An additional source for the preparation of MARC records for software is the *Machine-readable Data Files Format* (MRDF). With the exception of genre or subject, all the other desired points of access are provided in the records produced by using these two sources.

Subject Headings and Classification
Subject headings and classification should be applied to software according to the same criteria as other materials in the collection. While there are some special needs for access, software, like other media, should be mainstreamed into the collection in terms of subject headings and classification. Besides one's own subject policies, the basic source for advice on how to provide subject access to software is *Guidelines on Subject Access to Microcomputer Software*.

The primary focus of subject analysis should be on the specific topic or subject of the software, or the genre of the software. This main subject heading can then be combined with a form subdivision to indicate that the item is software. *Guidelines on Subject Access to Microcomputer Software* recommends the use of *Software* as the appropriate form subdivision. Individual libraries may choose to add subdivisions for the machine, operating system, programming

114

language, and age level or degree of difficulty. All of these exist in
the descriptive cataloging, and the system requirements may be made
accessible as an added entry in the 753 field. Separate entries should
not be made under *Computer software* or *Computer programs,* since such a
practice would produce unwieldy or ambiguous files that would intermix
all software as a form with general books about computer programs or
software.

        As in subject analysis, it is important that classification policy
is applied in the same manner for software as for other materials in
the collection. An accession number arrangement may seem convenient
when the software collection is small, but as the collection grows the
absence of classification removes a powerful tool of access for the
user. Likewise, classifying by form alone would collocate dissimilar
subjects together solely on the basis of being microcomputer software.

Catalog Access
        Given the information in the descriptive cataloging and subject
analysis, the last challenge in meeting users' needs is ensuring that
access is available to the contents of the catalog record. In an
online catalog, the contents of the title, author, title added entry,
author added entry, producer, subject, and call number fields are
usually accessible. Notes such as the system requirements note or
annotated notes may or may not be accessible depending on system design
and whether or not the MRDF format has been fully implemented. It may
or may not be possible to restrict a search to software by limiting it
to the MRDF materials type or by specifying the form subdivision
Software. A card catalog poses additional access problems since it
offers less flexibility in combining different access points in the
search process. It is a challenge to the designer of the catalog
record to take into consideration the needs of the user, sound
cataloging practices, and the limitations of one's catalog in order to
provide good subject access to microcomputer software.

References

American Library Association, Committee on Cataloging: Description and
        Access. *Guidelines for Using AACR2 Chapter 9 for Cataloging
        Microcomputer Software.* Chicago: ALA, 1984.

American Library Association, Subject Analysis Committee, ad hoc
        Subcommittee on Subject Access to Microcomputer Software.
        Guidelines on Subject Access to Microcomputer Software. Chicago:
        ALA, 1986.

Machine-readable Data Files Format. Dublin, Ohio: OCLC, 1984.

115

FROM LITTLE LEAGUE SYSTEM
TO MAJOR LEAGUE CORPORATE RESOURCE

(Development and Enhancement of a BRS Software-Based
Information Retrieval System)

Bonnie D. Montjar, Kennametal, Inc.

SUMMARY

The purpose of the Kennametal, Inc. Technology Information Center (TIC) is to locate, acquire, store, retrieve and distribute information in accord with the technical and business interests of the corporation. As a staff function within the Corporation, the TIC justifies its existence by the quality of service it provides. Since we are an integral part of the Corporate Technology Group, we felt that ours should not be merely an archival or "on demand" function. Rather, we saw that it would be to everyone's benefit for our staff to stay current with the research interests of Kennametal and participate pro-actively in furthering the objectives of corporate R & D. We provide information as requested, but also actively scan relevant literature, and pass along items of interest.

Throughout the brief history of the Technology Information Center, the management and staff have been committed to automating as many of the day-to-day functions as possible. This is because our users now depend on us for timely, relevant information   Automation of a number of administrative operations was perceived as a means of improving productivity, and increasing the level of service being offered. Productivity becomes increasingly important as other departments, hearing of the service we have provided to Corporate Technology, request our help.

Automation of the tasks that we targeted could be accomplished using text-based information retrieval software. This fact was recognized from the beginning of the analysis phase, with the result that our project was primarily software-driven. We identified several software packages that would address our needs. The problem with many of them was that they would not run on anything smaller than a minicomputer. Many of those packages that would run on smaller computers were "locked in" to micro-based operating systems, and could not migrate to larger computers if the need arose. Although we wanted to base our system on the correct software, we also had certain budget limitations, so the cost/benefit ratio had to be small. Another constraint was the fact that we were purchasing a corporate asset, and had to stay within a fairly narrow range of manufacturers of equipment. At the 1984 Integrated Online Library Systems Conference in Atlanta, I described the system that we initially assembled. The configuration, briefly, was based on an IBM PC/XT with a unique hardware upgrade from a company called Sritek in Cleveland, Ohio, which turned the XT into a multi-user system running UNIX [1].

We knew that the information retrieval software produced by BRS Information Technologies in Latham New York would run under UNIX on multi-user supermicrocomputers, and felt that   it *should* run on our experimental system. The BRS software would give us free-text searching of our records, variable length fields, variable length records, word was also a program available from Dartmouth College that would take the OCLC MARC records from our retrospective conversion, strip out the numeric field tags and put the records into BRS input format, with our own internally-defined field tags. This we intended to use to create an online book catalogue.

The major problem in getting any software, was the non-standard character of our system. BRS could not send us an off-the-shelf version, since they had no comparable machine to which to port the software. After much discussion, our hardware was transported to BRS's headquarters in Latham, New York, and Version 1.4 of the BRS Information Retrieval software was ported to and compiled on our system.

After extensive testing of the prototype, it became clear that a more dependable, more responsive system was necessary for a production type of environment. We needed to accomodate five simultaneous users on BRS without a decrease in performance. As before, two of our requirements were small cost/benefit ratio and compatibility with corporate standards. We wanted to stay with the BRS software, knowing that it could be migrated to progressively larger machines. The strongest reasons for keeping this path open were the possibility of putting our application on a mainframe, or becoming part of the corporate-wide local area network, to allow access to our data. As our project has received increasing attention, there have been requests from other departments for demonstrations of the system's capabilities and also access to our cataloguing records. Our upgrade has now, itself, become a prototype for a more widely used corporate resource.

When we received the approval to upgrade from our prototype, several options were open to us. Our creativity was tested, as we searched for hardware that would run our BRS software (off-the-shelf this time) and could, with minimum enhancement, accomodate our application for at least the next three years. The heaviest users of the system had to be reassured that similarity of operation in the upgrade would minimize disruption., Also, the new system had to be as "plain vanilla" and maintainable by the manufacturers, and software producers as possible. We had already researched the AT&T 3B2/300 and had concluded that it was one of several that would be a perfect fit for our application. With a 3B2, we could buy a standard BRS package, put the hardware in the same location as our PC-based machine, use all our existing cabling and all of our existing hardware. (The connections to the PC's that we would be using as terminals were already in place). The 3B2 would allow a relatively smooth transition from our original system.

Once the hardware was in place, the data had to be transferred from the old system to the 3B2. Despite the absence of a standard data conversion program, none of the data that we had already entered into our prototype was lost, thanks to the combined features of BRS, UNIX, and the file transfer capabilities of our terminal emulation software. Exhaustive testing proved that the transfer was successful. After a brief period of running the two systems in parallel, the switchover was made, and the 3B2 became our "administrative assistant".

[1] UNIX is a trademark of AT&T Bell Laboratories

117

A BULLETIN BOARD FOR ILL

Cathy Moore, Wisconsin Interlibrary Services

Across Wisconsin, TWX machines clattered bravely in the face
of fast-approaching, inevitable doom. Their time was up; we all
knew it. Yet they courageously cranked out thousands of ILL
requests from far-flung corners of the state, even while a task
force created by the state Division for Library Services plotted
their demise.

When the task force discovered a shareware bulletin board
program could cheaply and easily replace the TWX system, vastly
speeding up transmission and eliminating the costs of renting
specialized equipment, the elderly machines rattled their last.
Now bulletin boards throughout the state silently, cheaply, and
efficiently speed the transmission of ILL requests.

At Wisconsin Interlibrary Services, an ILL clearinghouse, we
run a bulletin board system (BBS) that's a modified version of the
one originally designed by WILS and state Reference and Loan
Library staff. Workers in 40 libraries use microcomputers to type
requests offline and send them over regular phone lines to our
board. While most requests are for WILS, callers also use the
board to send files directly to each other.

We get about 64,300 requests on the board each year (74% of
our total). It costs about 5 cents to send a request to the
bulletin board, while TWX costs averaged 80 cents and OnTyme II
electronic mail cost 40 cents per request.

Librarians calling the board need a microcomputer (IBM PCs
dominate), a modem, telecommunications software, and a program to
type requests. Although a few libraries use word processors, most
use specialized request formatting programs.

At WILS, we run RBBS-PC version 13.1 on an IBM PC with 640K
and a 10 megabyte hard disk. We got most of the board's software
for free: RBBS-PC is widely available as shareware, and we use
public domain utility programs downloaded from other boards. The
only program we bought was DoubleDOS, a multitasking program that
gave us another PC for $49. DoubleDOS divides the computer's
memory, letting you do two things at once. The bulletin board
handles calls in one section of memory, while we print requests
and use word processors and file managers in the other section.

The BBS is more than just a replacement for the TWX system.
When more callers to the board use the standard WILS format,
we'll be able to put our requests in a database and keep track of
them there. We've also begun to use the board to announce WILS
activities and distribute public domain programs useful in
libraries.

HOW IT WORKS

A librarian types requests offline, then uses a communications program and a modem to call the board. She enters her

library name, reads general bulletins and any messages for her, and then transfers files. She'll send her file to our disk; if we have a file for her, she'll download it. Then she logs off and prints her requests. The average call takes two to three minutes.

At noon and again at the end of the day, we print off the requests we've received so far and give them to student runners. In the afternoon, a student worker types the next day's requests and adds them to the board. None of the staff members who work with the board has had extensive microcomputer experience.

Because the board is easy to use, most librarians have been able to make do with a short manual. We haven't trained anyone in person, although we have helped callers once they're online: we can watch their work, enter commands for them, and even chat by typing. A caller in acute distress can page WILS staff by entering a command that makes our computer beep plaintively.

Bad phone lines and unsophisticated communications programs cause most of our few problems. Callers sometimes run into trouble when they first start using their computer, and several of our callers have little time to enter and send requests because their computers are heavily scheduled.

OTHER BOARDS

Wisconsin has four other ILL bulletin boards, with one more being planned. The BBS at the Nicolet Federated Library System in Green Bay is going well, with 11 callers when this was written. The board at the Southwest Wisconsin Library System was the first to use DoubleDOS; the system at the Reference and Loan Library gets calls from public libraries and systems all over the state. The BBS at Milwaukee Co. Federated Library System runs on a Compaq Deskpro with a hard disk. Finally, Linda Miller at Arrowhead Library System plans to set up an RBBS-PC board for ILL.

SETTING UP YOUR OWN BOARD

You could set up your own board for ILL or general library communications without much expense or trouble. You'll need a moderately powerful microcomputer with generous disk space, a modem that can answer the phone, a regular phone line, and a program like RBBS-PC that will handle calls and transfer files. You'll also need a staff member with microcomputer experience who has a lot of free time for the intitial installation.

For more information on setting up your own board, write to Cathy Moore, WILS, Room 464, 728 State St., Madison, WI 53706, or call the Madison IBM PC User Group BBS at 608-256-8088 and download and un-squeeze the file called BBSETUP.DQC.

119

Rachel Moreland, Kansas
State University Libraries

The space management program helps predict where and in what amounts space will be needed in the stacks. It also shows where space is being used, thus providing planning information for future shifts. Our program uses SuperCalc3 but it could be done with any relatively powerful spreadsheet software. We use two spreadsheets-- Spreadsheet #1 is for predictions and Spreadsheet #2 is for actual growth.

The illustration on the right shows the headings for these spreadsheets:

Each spreadsheet has two basic sections. The statistical information used for the calculations are on the left side and the calculated information is on the right. On Spreadsheet #1 the information includes: the total amount of shelf space available (TS); the total amount occupied(TOS); free space (FS); total growth inches (TGI); the total amount occupied space in each category at the beginning of the project (OS); the monograph average size (MAS) and the periodical average size (PAS); the projected growth rate in volume number of monographs (MGR) and of periodicals (PGR); and the projected growth in inches for monographs (MGI) and for periodicals (PGI).

On the growth spreadsheet a lower case "a" following the abbreviations denotes "actual".

The right side of each spreadsheet provides the projections
(on spreadsheet #1) or information on the actual growth (on
spreadsheet #2) at any given point in time. On the projection
spreadsheet the **Projected % of Growth** is the most crucial item
because the free space available is allotted to the individual
categories according to this ratio. **Available free space** plus
the occupied space in each category becomes the basis for
calculating the number of inches of empty **space that should be
left on each shelf.** Our program is designed so that ALL the
information for occupied space, growth rate, etc. must be input
BEFORE the number of inches to leave per shelf is accurate in any
of the categories.

This management program is only as good as the information
upon which it is based. We measured shelves to determine the
space available and measured books to determine shelf occupancy.
The latter measurements were totaled by categories based upon the
Library of Congress classifications. In the end the categories
were adjusted so none had less than 1000" of occupied space--an
amount felt to be large enough to make the calculations
meaningful.

The projected growth rate must be determined by working from
the library's archival information for a selected period of time.
This can be whatever period the library decides upon. However, it
should be long enough to show trends, since it is used to develop
the ratio that is the crucial figure in determining the free
space that is allotted to each category.

All columns with formulas are protected, as well as columns
with total space, classification categories, and average sizes.
Numbers then can only be entered in the columns for growth (MGR &
MGRa and PGR & PGRa). All the rest are calculated.

The monographic growth is kept current by using a
printout, contracted for with AMIGOS. It is based on the
library's OCLC archive tapes with the information in categories
that match those on the spreadsheets. The stacks supervisor
provides the periodicals growth information by tallying the
volumes received for shelving from the Binding Unit.

As long as **space available** and **occupied shelf space** is kept
accurate on the spreadsheets, they will be valuable management
tools.

COMPUTER SCHEDULING OF REFERENCE DESKS

Willy Owen, Davis Library, University of North Carolina

The problems of scheduling staff at reference desks are common to almost all libraries. Especially in large libraries, the process of scheduling a dozen or more librarians, support staff, and students to cover service hours is complex and time consuming. A schedule should pair inexperienced student workers with knowledgeable librarians. A schedule must also recognize that staff have other responsibilities that take them away from the desk for many hours during the day. Students' class schedules must be worked around. If one person's schedule changes--a student adds a new class, a librarian receives a time-consuming committee appointment--the desk schedule may need extensive revision.

Prior attempts have have been made to employ computers to schedule public service desks. DeHaas (1983) describes such a model, developed on a university-owned mainframe, but concludes that it may be as effective to produce the schedule by hand. The exigencies of personal preferences, which necessitate multiple computer runs, make mainframe programming an expensive solution. But with the advent of microcomputers and powerful applications software, it is now possible to design user-friendly programs, and to run those programs as often as desired without incurring on-going costs.

At the University of North Carolina, we began our search for a workable solution to the computerized scheduling of reference desks by contacting faculty in the Curriculum of Operations Research, with whom the library has successfully cooperated on other projects over the years. A graduate student, Jagdesh Mirchandani, produced a prototype program that will schedule up to twelve persons for service at the desk during weekday hours. The program uses Lotus 1-2-3, Release 2, for input and output. The schedule is solved using LP83, a linear programming package produced by Sunset Software. The ability to use linear programming is the key to the successful use of computers in this scheduling problem.

A linear programming model is a set of algebraic relationships comprised of two elements. The first is a mathematical description or enumeration of constraints which must be satisfied. In this case, constraints include the demand for staffing at various hours of the day, the number of desk hours to which someone may be assigned, and responsibilities that prevent assignment at any given hour. The second element is the criterion function which is to be optimized. The linear program selects a solution that is desirable, from among all possible solutions, according to an explicit criterion. Here the criterion function seeks to schedule staff according to their availability and their preferences, if any, for assignment. For example, students cannot be scheduled during hours when they have classes. Some staff prefer to work two-hour shifts at the desk, while others feel that they can provide better service if they are given a break from the desk after an hour.

122

The first step in producing the computerized model is the collection of data. These data include the hours which are to be scheduled, the number of staff on duty at the desk at each hour, and the total number of staff available for scheduling. In addition, the input includes an upper limit on the number of hours individuals can work at the desk, the specific hours they are available for assignment, and finally, any preferences they may express. The program can currently handle twelve staff members at a time. All staff are asked to provide a list of twenty weekday hours when they are available to work the desk, and to assign a preference rating (from one to five) to each hour.

Once all data have been collected they are input into a series of Lotus worksheets. The Lotus programs are macro-driven, and provide the user with a series of menus to facilitate data entry. The user is prompted for data at each step of the way, and is given the opportunity to edit data at any time during the input process. When all data have been entered, another Lotus macro creates a matrix which LP83 uses as input for the linear programming model.

LP83 uses long-tested methods that find, among all feasible solutions, one that best solves the problem according to the stated criterion. It does this is an extremely fast and efficient manner. On an IBM PC/AT equipped with a math coprocessor, LP83 solves the schedule in under two minutes.

The solution of the linear programming model is automatically inserted into another Lotus worksheet that prints the schedule. The first solution can be reviewed for appropriateness, and if changes are needed, the LP can be run again. An option in the Lotus input model allows the user to preschedule any individual in any time slot. In effect, the user can assign an individual to any given hour and subsequently run the LP model to establish the remainder of the schedule. The prescheduling option is also a simple way of giving priority to a particular staff member's requirements or preferences for scheduling.

The use of linear programming on microcomputers in this application points out how micros can play an important role in decision-making and in the allocation of resources within a library. The micro has already proven its worth as a tool for data management in the library environment; I believe that this model points the way to new administrative applications.

Reference

deHaas, Pat (1983, May 15). Computerizing the reference desk. Library Journal, 973-975.

"Using an Off-the-Shelf Online Catalog Package: Constraints -- No Compromises"

Annette Peretz, Bronx Community College
Frederick B. Low, Fiorello LaGuardia Community College

This presentation is the "log of a local catalog," describing how special needs can provide innovative solutions for small library catalogs.

The Learning Center at Bronx Community College is a model educational program serving about 7,000 non-traditional students with diverse learning needs. These students have ESL difficulties, basic skills deficiencies, lack conventional high school preparation; but present a high degree of motivation and determination to improve themselves via a college education.

The Learning Center's 10,000 item collection of videotapes, filmstrips, slidesets, audiocassettes, and, recently, microcomputer software, was developed more than 13 years ago to complement the curricula at the college. The correlation with courses is further reinforced through a program of referrals to the Learning Center by instructors. The mission of the Learning Center is to help students locate the specific program they need. Unlike books, audiovisual items are not "browsable" -- there are no tables of contents, indexes, etc., to help the user select the appropriate item. The specific finding mechanisms in use are: (a) an author-title-subject card catalog, (b) typewritten mediagraphies for all major courses (arranged on a 33-foot long program bulletin board), (c) professional librarian on reference duty at all times for one-on-one assistance. While mechanism "c" is, and always will be, an optimal means of information retrieval, "a" and "b" have major deficiencies. For example, obsolete card catalog headings such as "English language -- Orthography and spelling" for materials on spelling skills; summaries of no more than one or two sentences even for multi-part series 15 or 20 hours in length; mediagraphies out of date by one or two years that do not show recent acquisitions. The purpose of this project was to develop an online catalog system to replace the card catalog and the typewritten mediagraphies with enhanced, locally-oriented catalog records.

Until recently, online systems for small library collections were not financially feasible except as spin-offs from larger databases. As the major bibliographic computer systems developed in the 60's and 70's -- notable OCLC in Ohio -- libraries accepted the method of cooperative cataloging, based on a data code largely prescribed by the Library of Congress. Where networking among collections is important, this uniformity is highly desirable. Where special local requirements must be served, using a centralized national source is of little value. Original records must be created, with the ability to omit certain types of unnecessary information and greatly expand essential user information, such as subject headings, summaries, audience level, and department or course applications.

Our challenge, therefore, consisted of two components: (a) create the kind of data record which would be most appropriate to our users, and recatalog the entire 10,000 item collection, and (b) identify an online microcomputer system able to house our database and provide flexible, state of the art index retrieval to fields, including keyword access.

A Title III grant is currently funding a two year project to develop our "dream catalog." Work on recataloging the collection began in Fall 1985; by Summer 1986 an exhaustive search process had identified a computer system which seemed to be promising. The story which we will be telling at SCIL has a beginning and a middle, but no end -- hence, it is a "log." Our story is also a success story: in the course of adapting an off-the-shelf catalog package, we have been able to meet all of our priorities (no compromises) while keeping within financial limits of the project (constraints).

We will describe how we identified a much more natural system of subject terms than Library of Congress, how we developed special workforms to facilitate the recataloging, the search for a suitable software package, the use of a consultancy, the exercise of budgetary constraints for both hardware and software, the selection of the off-the-shelf package, and arrangements for customizing of this package.

At this time data entry of cartons of workforms is proceeding apace. As soon as a subject collection is completed, pilot testing of that portion will start, because customizing arrangements enable us to make changes up to the final version.

We believe that what we are doing will make a difference in precision of access and in user satisfaction. We also believe that if others with similar needs knew that local catalogs to meet individual needs were not beyond budgets and effort, many would choose to improve access rather than to accept conformity as inevitable.

125

USING UNIX FOR LANS AND BULLETIN BOARDS

Phillip E. Rose, AT&T Technical Library

The hardware core of our LAN and bulletin board is an AT&T 3B2/300 multiuser supermicrocomputer that links our AT&T PC6300, MS-DOS microcomputers to it via PC Interface. PC Interface is the LAN hardware and software that interconnects the 3B2 with any IBM-compatible personal computer. In addition, UNIX System V is available as a general purpose, multi-user, multi-tasking, interactive operating system. UNIX, which provides LAN users with file serving and spooling, also provides a sophisticated writing tool, "writers workbench," used to prepare this summary. Access to "UNIX Newsnets," online subject interest groups throughout AT&T, is made possible through UNIX on the 3B2. Because these nets are widely read, much of our Library's public relations effort is directed at putting up bulletins and notices on them.

The 3B2 acts as the UNIX core of our LAN, serving as a link between PC work stations not only in the Library but, also in Engineering Records, one isle down from us. I have six AT&T PC6300s and one PC clone from Bibliofile, tied into the LAN. They are all configured for top performance. Each machine has 640K of RAM, five have a 20Mg and one has a 10Mg hard disk, all have extra serial ports (for PC INTERFACE). Additionally, the Bibliofile work station has a CD-ROM, used both for acquisitions and as a CD library for the bulletin board. PC Interface provides our two literature searchers with access to a high speed dot matrix printer for quick search output to our customers. It also provides any work station with the use of our only letter quality printer. The PC work stations are used for the following purposes; literature searching, acquisitions, purchase orders, vouchers, word processing/editing, serials and database management, calculators and as UNIX terminals. Every library staff member has been encouraged to think of tasks they perform manually, that would benefit from the use of the LAN to enhance their efficiency and enable us to better serve our customers.

Our 3B2 is also the home of an equally important project, the AT&T TECHNICAL LIBRARY BULLETIN BOARD. We have followed AT&T UNIX protocols and named this dial-up machine, drbul. My goal for drbul, is to bring together PC users, who because of our building's size (1.3 million square feet), could not easily get together to share programs, ideas and questions. The bulletin board serves its subscribers by acting as a multi-user (up to eight at one time), distributor MS-DOS software. Several different organizations in the building including; the Laboritories, manufacturing engineering, the marketing and services organizations, and my administrative group, regularly download this software. However drbul, was also conceived as a place for interaction between the "BBS Team" and our user community. This team consisting of me, our PC Coordinator, the Office Automation Coordinator, our PC Trainer, and the 3B2/PC6300 Network Coordinators, acts as online expert consultants on a variety of PC related problems. PC users can leave questions for team members on drbul, rather than playing phone tag with people who are often away from their desks consulting.

Biographical note: Victor Rosenberg

Victor Rosenberg is President and founder of Personal Bibliographic
Software, Inc. and Associate Professor of Information and Library Studies
at the University of Michigan. After receiving his master's degree in
information science from Lehigh University and a doctorate from the
University of Chicago, he spent six years teaching at the University of
California at Berkeley. PBS, Inc. develops and markets software for
information professionals and researchers.

Executive Summary:

Software for Library Applications -- A Developer's Point of View

The special characteristics of library microcomputer applications
requires a careful attention to detail. Although many librarians try to
adapt general purpose or business software, most library problems are
just different enough to demand specialized solutions. The library market
also places specific demands on vendors. Issues of user training,
copyright restrictions, support for users, and the continuing nature of
software development will be discussed. Five years of experience in
selling software to librarians forms the background for the presentation.

Acquiring and Using Shareware in Building Small Scale Automated
Information Systems

Alan R. Samuels Ph.D.
School of Library and Informational Science
University of Missouri-Columbia

Small libraries and other information agencies often
cannot afford to develop in-house automated information
systems. Larger libraries, while richer, are generally
reluctant to undertake similar projects because of
restrictive software licensing agreements coupled with the
enormous expense of multiple copy software purchases for
each part of what might be a very decentralized system.
Although libraries have usually been among the first to
adopt automation, whatever exist tend to be closely tied to
traditional library functions (such as reference) or used
for stock management (such as automated circulation
systems). Expense, therefore, can restrict creativity.

Developing small scale automated information systems
(SSAIS) in economically restrictive environments can be done
through the use of alternative products. While such
products are not likely to replace deeply entrenched,
standardized, and institutionalized hardware/software
configurations (OCLC terminals and software, for example),
they can be used to develop new and innovative services in
those areas where standardization and replication are not
serious issues but budgetary considerations are.

Software is the most important part of a SSAIS.
Hardware is not a major consideration since fiscal
restraints will force system developers to utilize older
(and hence cheaper) technology. The variety of surrogate
inexpensive hardware available to the buyer who is willing
to accept less than the very latest is astonishing.

It is software that is often the most expensive and
least understood part of the SSAIS. Many computer-wise
librarians tend to equate utility with expense and size:
the longer the documentation and the greater the expense the
more useful a program is thought to be. While acknowledging
the existence of smaller, cheaper, and less complex software
products, they rarely understand nor use them. The stronger
this attitude is, the more are librarians prone to acquire
extremely powerful, sophisticated, and expensive software
that they really do not need nor can possible use to
anything approaching its full potential. A major way of
reducing software anxiety is to carefully describe your
actual application needs, not adopt the perspectives of over
zealous vendors.

Problems like those outlined above can be avoided by
recognizing that there is at least as much diversity in
software as in hardware. At present software can be divided
into three basic categories:

I. Level One: Commercial products - products sold through
retail stores and by mail order houses. Most software used
is of this type. It is characterized by highly restrictive
licensing agreements and is usually, though not always,

129

quite expensive. Most large packages and multipurpose
software are in this category

II. <u>Level Two:</u> Public domain products - software developed
by individual programmers which is released for unrestricted
use "in the public domain." Public domain software usually
copyright in order to prevent its <u>not</u> being made freely
available. Quality control in public domain software varies
widely. Most programs in this category are of the utility
type although programs of every type can be found.

III. <u>Level Three:</u> Shareware products - software developed
by individual entrepreneurs and distributed through non-
traditional ways (such as remote bulletin boards and through
computer clubs). Shareware software is itself divided into
several levels ranging from virtually no restrictions on use
to requirements bordering on those found in commercial
software licensing agreements.

Shareware programs are the most likely candidates for
inclusion in a SSAIS. Many products currently available
commercially began their journey toward through the
shareware route. Pursuing this method of distribution
allows an author to continually refine and evolve a program.
Users who obtain copies of the program are asked to provide
a small contribution (sometimes called a "donation,"
sometimes a "registration fee). In return, users are sent
updated versions or other rewards for registering.

Unlike public domain programs (which shareware is most
emphatically not), shareware programs can be highly
sophisticated yet easy to use ways of simplifying SSAIS
tasks at very minimal expense. Many types of software not
represented in the public domain area can be found among
shareware. This includes AI systems, relational database
management systems, 3-dimensional spreadsheets, and similar
exotica.

Acquiring <u>current</u> versions of shareware software is
often much more difficult than one might suspect. The best
source are remote bulletin boards maintained by individuals
or groups. Of the hundreds of such RBBs only a few are
worth continual surveillance. Knowing specific titles of
programs to look for is also difficult because there is no
existing source at present that provides adequate critical
reviews of these products. However, opinions can often be
gleaned from computer clubs and other unofficial sources as
well as from some commercial public domain and shareware
distributing organizations. Careful scanning of trade
newsletters, journals, and the classified sections of major
journals can also provide useful access points.

Executive Summary
Graphics Processing on the Microcomputer:
Digitizers and their Application to Libraries.
Scott Seaman

This paper reviews microcomputer digitizers and examines the
possibilities for library application. Digitizers are hardware that
copy printed materials or video images and create machine-
readable files from them. The image can then be enhanced or
resized with the digitizer's software, stored in graphic form, or
moved directly to a text document to be used as an illustration.

Digitizers enable librarians to add clarity and interest to
documents. Transferring graphics can be done quickly and without
specialized training in computer techniques. The librarian controls
the content, the speed, delivery, quantity, quality, and form of
the images. The digitizer, then, is a tool to efficiently transfer
and communicate complex information.

The most significant limitation of microcomputer digitizers is
that images are stored as bitmapped files rather than as objects.
Because of this, digitized images must be edited dot by dot.
Digitized text, for example, cannot be edited with a wordprocessor.

While the hardware surveyed operates with Apple's Macintosh,
comparable software is available for MS-DOS based microcomputers.

USING MICROCOMPUTERS TO TRAIN LIBRARY STAFF

Suzanne J. Shaw, University of Florida Libraries

Libraries have thus far used microcomputers mainly for word processing, spreadsheets and other off-the-shelf applications. There is very little library-specific software available. Software publishers have been uninterested in relatively small, "vertical markets" such as libraries, so librarians must develop their own software to meet their own needs.

Getting staff involved with micros is best accomplished by hands-on experience with software that can demonstrate ways to do things better and more efficiently than other methods. Most professionals recognize the value of word processing; it obviously helps with reports, memos, correspondence and other professional responsibilities. Similarly, spreadsheets take much of the pain out of budgeting and statistics. For support staff, however, use of computer-assisted instruction (CAI) either to train them in a library function, or help them train others, can be a more pragmatic introduction to the technology.

CAI in libraries has mostly been oriented toward bibliographic instruction of the library end user. The potential for use in staff training, while largely unexplored, is enormous. There are many clerical library tasks, particularly in technical services, that must be taught repeatedly to student assistants or clerks. A number of these could be taught better and more thoroughly by computer.

A successful CAI is one that takes advantage of the unique characteristics of a computer: patience (the computer never gets tired or bored); variety (a large number of examples can be presented in random order); speed (the lessons can proceed as fast or slow as the individual finds comfortable). Good CAI utilizes a large amount of interaction, presents a challege, rewards success and offers encouragement.

The experience of the University of Florida with a CAI developed in-house, "How To Search OCLC," is instructive. It took three times longer than expected to develop, but has been used to an extent far beyond any expectation. Literally hundreds of students and permanent library staff at all levels have been trained at UF, and it has been used in all types of libraries across the U.S., Canada and the Caribbean. Its developers believe that most potential CAI applications are less generic, and that less ambitious programs could be created using authoring languages such as

Logo while still retaining the elements that make CAI such
an interesting and valuable training tool.

THE PLEASURES AND PERILS OF APPLE IIe ENHANCEMENT IN A SMALL LIBRARY

Sally S. Small, Berks Campus, Pennsylvania State University

The original microcomputer system was a 64K DOS 3.3 Apple IIe equipped with double disk drives, an 80 Column Text Card, an Epson RX-80 printer with parallel interface card, and an Apple Super Serial card. The system was a backup unit for the microcomputer laboratory which was "loaned" to the library in September, 1983. It came with no software. Today it is an enhanced IIe with a 256K expandable RamWorks card, a 1200 baud modem, and an Apple Daisywheel printer in addition to the Epson FX-85 printer. A second unit with a 1 MEG RamWorks card is dedicated to circulation. Each tiny step in the enhancement process was achieved in spite of a lack of knowledge, product information, and money. AppleWriterII, AppleWorks, ReportWorks, ASCII Express, and Print Shop are now used to perform many routine library tasks. The presentation will include the steps taken, the problems encountered, and the remedies achieved in the maturing of these Apples.

The library serves a branch campus of a major state university and is a part of that university's library system. The two budget sources, the campus administration and the library system, could not be relied on for funds to purchase equipment, library software, or for development of "temporary" microcomputer applications.

The opportunity to use microcomputers came in September, 1983 with a request from the Academic Dean at the Campus for a secure space in the library for students to use five Apple IIe's during all hours of library operation. These five were the 'backup' units for the 10 installed in the computer laboratory. He stated that these were intended for student use, but could be used for library tasks when not in use by students. Educational software packages, supplied by the few faculty members who planned to use microcomputer units in their courses, were placed on reserve and the library was in the microcomputer public access business overnight.

The constraints to development of library applications included a lack of interest and financial support from the University Libraries and the campus administration, lack of campus personnel trained in microcomputer technology or use, lack of library staff experience with microcomputers, and an obsolete telephone system with all receivers directly wired and a central switchboard.

Word processing was the first priority. The Head Librarian had used AppleWriterII and pursuaded the academic dean to purchase it for library reserve with the understanding that she would help students learn to use it. The student assistants who were interested in learning were assigned repetitive tasks including the preparation of duplicate exchange lists, The Periodical Holdings List, mailing labels and form letters. Staff members learned to word process in self defense as students pleaded with them for help. All staff members use AppleWriterII and all major or repetitive typing tasks are now completed on the Apple.

134

The Epson RX-80 printer, although highly efficient and durable, was not adaptable to single feed forms and sheets, and copy was not letter quality. A Daisywheel printer was purchased with fiscal year end funds drawn from the Dean's and the library's supply budgets.

Print Shop was acquired when a student computer advocate 'gave' a staff member a copy of this neat little program. The staff tried it, liked it, and bought it. The next year the supply requisition included colored ribbons and colored pin feed paper to brighten up signs and announcements posted in the library building.

Achieving telecommunications capability was a more difficult task. The Dean loaned the library a 1200 baud Racal-Vadic acoustic modem which was no longer needed in the computer laboratory. ASCII Express software was purchased because our colleagues at the local community college were using it successfully with Apple IIe equipment. A computer-wise student undertook the task of fitting these pieces together to enable the staff to access the library's on-line system, the computer center's mainframe computer, and the commercial databases. Many months, letters, and phone calls later the 1200 baud modem was scrapped for a TRS 300 baud acoustic modem which kept lines connected through the campus switchboard. The staff was online at last.

A new campus-wide phone system installed early in 1985 included a jack in the library for a modem and the summer of 1986 the Reference Librarian saved sufficient funds from a professional development grant to purchase a 1200 baud U. S. Robotics Password Modem. The new modem is more efficient and with ASCII Express answers the needs. Best of all the captured files can be edited with AppleWriter.

A part-time evening assistant introduced the library staff to AppleWorks. She saw applications the staff could not see and encouraged all to try. The Head Librarian attended a one day seminar on AppleWorks at a local computer store. The Data Base label printing format appeared to be the solution to the multipart forms that the library system requires and requests typed letter perfect. Templates were designed for two 3"x5" multipart preprinted order forms. The limited 64K memory spawned many small files, but the procedures worked and solved not only typing problems, but also tracked expenditures. The next summer (1986) a 256K RamWorks card was purchased to solve the memory problem. The 5"X 8" lending forms were more difficult to produce, because the printed lines required exceeded the limits of the Data Base label format. ReportWorks was purchased and a template designed to print these larger forms.

Problems continue to plague the development. A switch of printers with the computer laboratory substituted an Epson FX-85 for the RX-80 and resulted in the loss of the adjustable pin-feed mechanism required for the five inch wide forms. ReportWorks would not run on the standard IIe. It required an enhanced unit. The ASCII Express software would not run on the enhanced IIe. These problems have been solved. The most pressing problems now are static electricity and scheduling a computer.

135

FOR REFERENCE ASSISTANCE...STRIKE ANY KEY

Dana E. Smith, Purdue University, W. Lafayette, IN

This paper explores the use of uniquely developed microcomputer programs to provide reference and directional service support to patrons at all times that the library is open, but intended to support service at times when reference personnel are not available.

The reference "Information Station" programs allow patrons to query specific subjects of interest or receive general building directories through interaction with the computer. Through utilization of a menu process of responses, program use generates a series of statistical summaries which can be used for management decision purposes. Each response or selection records to a file the nature of interaction with the programs. In this respect, information can be acquired regarding heavy use subjects, total number of interactions at the date and time of day the query was made, and whether or not the user of the program received adequate information. This is determined through analysis of the particular track the patron used reflected in the following example of a statistical table output summary.

STATISTICAL TABLE

	Y P	Y Q	Y R	Y S	N P	N Q	N R	N S	T Y	T N
-0	0	0	0	1	0	0	0	0	1	0
-1	0	0	0	0	0	0	0	0	0	0
-2	0	1	1	0	0	3	1	0	2	4
-3	1	0	0	1	2	0	1	0	2	3
-4	0	1	0	0	0	0	0	0	1	0
-5	4	4	0	0	1	3	2	0	8	6
-6	(tallies continue through path 87)									
88	5	6	1	2	3	6	4	0	14	13

(row 88 contains total for each column)

NOTES ON THE STATISTICAL TABLE:

For Rows 1 through 88
The first four columns show times when the person's question was answered. The second four columns show times when the person's question was not answered.

P means the person subsequently called the previous menu
Q means the person quit
R means the person returned to the main menu
S means the person called the suggestion box

An important additional aspect of the Information
Station program offerings is the capability for a user to
call the Suggestion Box program at any time in the interactive process. If a user does not discover needed information, he/she can call the Suggestion Box program to input
the nature of their question and/or the suggestion they
might have. This allows several advantages for users and
library managers. Information recorded in the Suggestion
Box file accounts for those areas of interest not reflected
in previously used programs and offers a methodology for
further contact with users that have been unable to interact
with reference personnel. The Suggestion Box file can be
printed at any time and will reveal the process used by a
patron prior to the calling of this program. Having information about times of interaction or what subject interest
an individual attempted can be helpful in development of
future program design. The following is an example of the
printed output of the Suggestion Box file.

SUGGESTION BOX

Time-	1520	Path-	26	Column-	3
Time-	1520	Path-	35	Column-	3
Time-	1520	Path-	7	Column-	1
Time-	1521	Path-	7	Column-	5
Time-	1521	Path-	7	Column-	5
Time-	1521	Path-	7	Column-	4

7
I need to find something on a painter
named Rembrandt Peale?

Dana
494-6729

The data collected from the Statistical Table and
Suggestion Box files provide management with information to
assist in collection development and planning library services.
Analysis of this data will reveal what are areas of interest,
the concentration of use of the library, and an ability to
learn of user's special interests.

The incorporation of microcomputer support programs
for this purpose can prove to be a valuable alternative to
individualized/personalized attention. These programs afford
a flexible, inexpensive alternative to meet demands for
service when reference personnel are too busy or unavailable.

137

HARD DISK ORGANIZATION AND MANAGEMENT

Lynn R. Smith, Indiana University School of Medicine Library

An IBM or compatible microcomputer with an organized hard disk is a powerful tool. The emphasis here must be on the word organized. An unorganized or a poorly organized disk is inefficient and difficult to use. On an unorganized hard disk, user files, DOS files, the files that make up applications software packages are filed randomly on the disk. Trying to find one particular file among a hundred randomly arranged files is time consuming. Updating to a new version of a software package which may involve removing the multiple files that comprised the older version can be tedious. When the computer has multiple users the problems caused by an unorganized disk are multiplied. On an organized disk, DOS files can be separated from other files, each software package can be separated from all other software packages, and user files can be separated in a variety of ways such as by user, or by type of file.

Although a hard disk has considerable storage space, when word processors, spreadsheet, and database management programs, to name a few, are installed, it does not take long to fill up the disk. Therefore, an essential part of using a hard disk is monitoring the files on it. If each user can easily pull up a directory listing of only his/her files created with a particular software package rather than a directory of all files on the disk regardless of user or type of file, it is much easier for that user to monitor, back-up, or delete files as needed. Making consistent and regular back-ups to floppy disk greatly lessens the always disastrous potential of disk failure.

The key to hard disk organization is the MS-DOS directory structure. In DOS, a directory is a file or group of files which is separated from all other files on the same disk or drive. The DOS directory structure is hierarchical in nature and allows multiple levels of directories, for example one directory can have subdirectories, which in turn can have subdirectories and so on. On an organized disk, the DOS files may be in one directory. A word processor may be installed in a second directory, with user files created by that word processor in a sub-directory of the first word processor directory. A spreadsheet program may be in a third directory with one user's spreadsheet files in a sub-directory and a second user's files in a another sub-directory of the spreadsheet program directory as shown below.

EXAMPLE OF HARD DISK DIRECTORY STRUCTURE

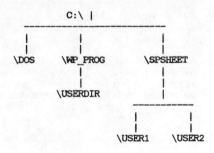

138

Although DOS can handle multiple levels of directories not all commercial software can. A software package can be set up to default into a particular directory for user files. However, if that software has multiple users who have separate directories for their files, it can be difficult and depending on the software occasionally impossible to access more than one directory. However, in addition to the directory structure, MS-DOS allows the hard disk to be partitioned into more than one drive designation. The hard disk is usually designated as drive C:, but it can be further divided into drives D:, E:, and F:. The partitioning of the hard disk is a step that must be done when the disk is initially installed. By partitioning the hard disk into more than one drive, (for example installing software in drive C: and designating drive D: for data files) software can be "outsmarted" into working with multiple directories.

Although there is no substitute for learning the necessary steps and DOS commands, commercial software is available to help keep track of hard disk files. In-house batch files can also be used to great advantage in manipulating through directories. A batch file is series of DOS commands that can be invoked through entering a single character or word. The use of a computer with a hard disk organized for multiple users can be greatly simplified with a few batch files. A set of batch files can be used to create a menu listing all the software installed on the disk. The menu batch files can be set up to default each user into their own directories for the software being used.

Understanding the DOS directory structure and learning to manipulate files on an organized hard disk can be difficult for some users particularly the inexperienced. However, trying to use a hard disk which is not organized can be difficult and tedious for even the experienced user.

L.Smith 1/5/86

DB Master VERSION FIVE:

HIGH PERFORMANCE DATA BASE MANAGEMENT

ON AN APPLE // MICROCOMPUTER

Barney Stone, Stone Edge Technologies, Inc.

There are many applications for microcomputer-based information management within the library environment. In general terms, there are two categories of software for performing these tasks: *special purpose* programs, meaning those written specifically for use in libraries, and *general purpose* programs which can be configured for use in a wide variety of applications.

Special purpose programs, also known as "vertical market" programs, have the advantage of being written and supported by specialists in a particular field. However, they tend to have two major disadvantages: they rarely incorporate the latest advances in either hardware or software, since their limited market makes them less attractive to the more sophisticated software developers; and they force users of the programs to manage their information in specific ways and formats which may not produce the best results in all cases.

General purpose programs, on the other hand, offer greater flexibility, but at a cost: they are frequently more difficult to use, and they may not be able to accomodate application-specific requirements, such as interfacing with a bar code reader.

Also, until recently, programs with the power, performance and flexibility needed for many applications were not available for the Apple // line of computers, forcing many users to limit their uses of the computer, to deal with inadequate or inconvenient software, or to switch to other, more expensive systems.

One general purpose program which has been used successfully in libraries is DB Master. A new version of the program, called DB Master Version Five, has recently been introduced. This new version takes advantage of some of the improvements made on the Apple // in recent years, and addresses and corrects many of the weaknesses of the program's earlier versions. For instance, it now includes "relational" capabilities, enabling it to work with more than one file at a time; its text handling capabilities have been vastly improved; and it can now be used with any ProDOS compatible disk drive.

These improvements and many others make DB Master Version Five a much more useful tool. The author will demonstrate the program, and discuss its use in library applications.

WHY & HOW TO IMPLEMENT A MULTIPLE FILE APPLICATION
USING dBASE III

Natalie Oakes Sturr
State University of New York College at Oswego

Effective library database management applications
often require the use of multiple files. Dividing data
among two or more files can reduce the amount of data needed
to be entered, edited and stored. Multiple files result in
better and faster access to information while conserving
disk space, reducing the possibility of "dirty" data, and
reducing personnel time needed to maintain the application.
To illustrate these concepts, a two file dBase III application which provides author and subject access to a collection will be examined.

For each item in the collection a single author, title
and an unlimited number of subject headings is recorded. A
unique code is assigned to each item to serve as a link
between the two files. Each record in the bibliographic
file contains author, title and other bibliographic information along with the code. There is one record in the file
for each item in the collection. Each record in the subject
file contains one subject heading and the code representing
the item to which the heading is assigned. There is one
record for each subject heading assigned to each item.

Records are added to the database by APPENDing information to both files and generating a unique code. The code
may be generated by first SAVEing a number in a dBase .MEM
file and then RESTOREing it within the program. The number
is incremented as needed and SAVEd to the .MEM file.

To print a list by subject, the subject file is
arranged be subject heading and the bibliographic file by
code. Beginning with the first record in the subject file,
the subject heading is printed. The code in the record is
stored, looked up in the bibliographic file, and the corresponding bibliographic information printed. The program
returns to the subject file, SKIPs to the next record and
repeats the process.

An author list is printed similarly. The bibliographic
file is arranged by author and the subject file arranged by
code. After the bibliographic information is printed, the
code is looked up in the subject file. After the subject
heading is printed, the next record in the subject file is
examined. If the code in the subject record matches the
code from the bibliographic record, the subject heading is
printed. This continues until the codes no longer match.

141

The appropriate record must be located whether editing or deleting information. Locating and displaying a record on the screen is similar to printing the lists. Rather than print entries consecutively, the appropriate entry in the first file is found with the SEEK command. Editing or changing information is done with the REPLACE...WITH command and deleting is done, preferably, with the DELETE and PACK commands.

Programming is an art, whether in dBase or an upper-level language such as PASCAL. The ideas presented here are not the only means of implementing a multiple file application. Hopefully the ideas provide basic information which will assist the reader in tailoring a particular application to a specific need.

OFFICE AUTOMATION: LESSONS LEARNED AT A&M

Janet Swanbeck, Librarian, Texas A&M University

More than two years ago, the Sterling C. Evans Library at Texas A&M University plunged into office automation by purchasing IBM PC's and software for word processing applications for every department. Since that time, emotions surrounding office automation have ranged from wild enthusiasm to intense frustration. The enthusiasm was predictable. The causes of frustration were frequently surprises, surprises which I can hopefully spare other libraries by sharing the lessons learned at Texas A&M.

Our original plan for a phased-in approach to office automation died when the library received a large sum of money which had to be used immediately for the purchase of microcomputers and peripherals. In retrospect, the gradual introduction of microcomputers would have been less traumatic to the library staff. The purchase of several microcomputers, software packages, and printers at one time did, however, result in a substantial discount. Our selection of IBM PC's was based on expandability, availability on state contract, and reputation. Dual disk drives seemed adequate then, but we are now purchasing only hard disk microcomputers. Networking was not a major consideration but is now being discussed.

The software needs identified by the individual units were varied. Word processing was, by far, the most popular choice followed by a spread sheet and data base manager. In the end, Word Star was purchased for each unit. This package was the most popular at the time and one for which we could easily find a trainer. Spread sheets and data base manager programs were purchased at a later date.

Training has been and continues to be the most debated issue surrounding office automation at Sterling C. Evans Library. Library staff quickly recognized the need for an on-going training and support program. The implementation of such a program involved creative planning in these times of tight budgets in Texas. We are now in the enviable position of having a librarian whose more than full-time responsibilities include training as well as assisting staff with software related problems.

In the fall of 1985, the library learned its hardest lesson. Two microcomputers disappeared within one month from the technical services area. We had neglected to provide for security and paid for this omission. We have since cabled the PC's to tables and have not experienced another theft.

Changes brought about by office automation continue to surface. Every department now looks for student workers with a major in Computing Science. Work areas have become crowded because of the enormous amount of space taken up by our computer furniture. When the noise levels became intolerable, baffles were ordered. Training now takes place in a separate room and there will soon be 20 IBM PC's in this facility.

Office Automation is now a fact of life at Sterling C. Evans Library. In retrospect, it seems miraculous that we were able to implement office automation in such a short period of time. Those of us who viewed its arrival with some apprehension have long since forgotten those early fears.

STAFFING ISSUES: HOW TO MANAGE CHANGE AND PROVIDE APPROPRIATE SUPPORT AFTER IMPLEMENTATION

Marnie Swanson, University of Calgary Libraries

INTRODUCTION

Many libraries are now using microcomputers to accomplish a variety of administrative and bibliographic tasks. The University of Calgary Libraries have been using microcomputers for such tasks for five years, with significant developments beginning in 1985. Currently microcomputers are used for: word processing; management of capital inventory; management of supplementary personnel and financial systems; control of the lending side of inter library loans; communications; and specialized collections databases. There are sixteen microcomputers operational throughout the library, all of which are IBM compatible and seven software packages are in use.

INTEGRATION

o   Management – the beginning stages of the project (i.e. hardware/software selection, procurement, and initial setup) were managed centrally. Since implementation, however, management of the project has been one of co-ordination rather than tight central control. Each Department has responsibility for the development of their individual applications with central help provided in the areas of quality control, training, trouble shooting, technical support, and on-going hardware/software evaluation. Staff have reacted well to this decentralized approach and many locally initiated innovations have been adopted system wide.

o   Staff Attitudes – the majority of the staff were already computer literate having used the on-line catalogue DOBIS for five years. In general, the attitudes were very positive with only a few expressing some reluctance to the changes. Expectations, however, were unrealistically high and had to be tempered in the beginning. In an attempt to reduce post implementation problems, staff participation was actively solicited throughout all the planning stages. Open communication and a free flow of information were factors that also contributed to the success of the project.

o   Technical Support – since implementation, essential technical support has been provided by a senior support staff member who has been assigned to the project on a half time basis. Without this support, the project would probably have floundered shortly after implementation. In a project of this size, it is crucial to have at least one person charged with the responsibility of dealing with equipment failures, software problems, on-going training, and applications development. At the University of Calgary, some technical support is also provided through the Departments of Computing Services and Administrative Systems.

145

o   Training - a necessary ingredient in any automation project is
     effective staff training.   Formal in-house training sessions
     have been offered, providing staff with introductory courses
     on the Zenith microcomputer, DOS, and DW3.   Individuals
     skilled in the use of specific software have provided informal
     training sessions on an as needed basis.   In addition, staff
     are encouraged to participate in microcmputer training courses
     offered by external agencies.

o   Policies - soon after implementation, it was agreed by
     Management that policies dealing with all aspects of the
     microcomputer project had to be developed and documented.
     Since no clear guidelines existed that articulated the Library's
     overall microcomputer philosophy, staff were often unclear on
     issues such as: how to proceed with new applications; the
     kind of technical support they could expect; the acquisition
     of new hardware and software; the development of in-house
     software vs purchasing off-the-shelf software, etc.   Work has
     now begun on the development of policies that deal with:
     acquisition of equipment; training, in-house technical
     support; data administration; microcomputer use; and
     evaluation of hardware and software.   Guidelines will also be
     developed that outline the recommended procedures to be used
     in the daily operation of the microcomputers.

CONCLUSION

At the University of Calgary, microcomputers are now an accepted
and integral part of many staff member's daily routines.   They have
very quickly embraced the technology and frequently propose innovative
new applications.   The challenge for the future will be to try to meet
the demand for new hardware and software in a time of fiscal restraint.

A SOFTWARE LENDING COLLECTION
R. S. Talab, Kansas State University

The development and maintenance of a software lending collection requires careful consideration of many aspects: "backups" (archival copies), licensing agreements, the enforceability of "shrink-wrap" contracts, security, reserve copies, acquisition policies, license negotiation, circulation, the liability of the librarian, and the development of copyright pollcies. Workable procedures will develop when usage practices, the demands of the marketplace, and a testing in the courts "flesh" out proper policies.1

Prior to ordering software the librarian should, whenever possible, determinc what license agreement pertains to a given software package. Each producer has varying practices. It might also be a good idea to inform the producer in writing on the conditions under which the library intends to make the software available with a standard statement, "for library lending purposes" (in-house, off campus, etc.), as well as a statement about the library's precautions against illegal copying (circulation cards signed by the patron, warnings afixed to the disk, the carrier, on the microcomputer, at the desk, etc.).

An archival copy should be requested when purchasing software. Most large companies provide one as a part of the package or at a nominal charge. While the number of producers supplying backups has risen, many still believe that these backups are used as second copies of a program instead of as archival copies, so they do not send a backup.2

The law states that a program;'s purchaser may make or have an archival copy made to guard against damage.3 The law is unclear, however, as to who is responsible for supplying the backup--the producer or the purchaser.4 The archival copy is to be used in the event of dmamage to the original, not to extend the life of the program or as a second copy.

Another area of concern are "shrinkwrap" licenses, so called because they are considered applicable when the purchaser opens the shrinkwrap. They may restrict copying, and many require that the software ve used on one machine or at one site. Except for the archival copy, such restrictions are the publishers' perogative. Two companies were sucessfully sued for multiple copies and multiple loading and an action against a school district was filed (later withdrawn) for the same reasons. While the reason for the shrinkwrap agreement is the acceptable reason that the prodcuer wishes to prevent extreme liablity, legal experts disagree as to the efficacy of such a test in the courts.5

Security of software is a major concern. Copyright warnings should be posted on disks, carriers, microcomputers and at the circulation desk. While such notices can reduce liability they will not eliminate it.

Disks placed on reserve by faculty and/or staff should be accompanied by a sheet which the faculty person signs that attests to the copies being made legally

While software checkout is being sucessfully implemented in public, academic, and school libraries, such practices depend on the patron, the software, and the setting. It might be wise to have the patron sign a circulation card which includes 1) information on the legal use of copyrighted programs, 2) a policy statement on such use on the part of the library, 3) a statement concerning charges should a disk be returned damaged, and 4) a statement that the student in the university, the student and his/her parents in a school setting, or the patron in the public setting will abide by copyright regulations and assume full responsiblity for checkout and use of such programs. In-house checkout of programs in a microcomputer center using a student I.D. card or the use of a network system might be preferable.

Whenever possible it is wise to either order programs that are copy protected or to use a locking program (such as Pro-Lock). While virtually every program can be copied, the use of such a device as a standard procedure would reduce library liability to some extent.

Should a court action be instituted, the librarian, the librarian, the department head and the institution would likely all be named in the suit.6 If the librarian loaned a software package and overheard the patron say that he/she would copy it then he/she could be a contributory infringer.7 A recent suit against a school district came about because software companies were surveyed by the ICIA (International Communications Industries Association which represents smaller software developers) about which school districts were suspected of copying software. Those districts at the top of the survey were then investigated. The district chosen had no policy. While the action did not go to court, one of the stipulations for settlement was that the district educate its teachers and students about ethical software use and draw up policies. This was also the case when New York University was sued for copyright infringement involving print materials and off-campus copying. NYU was one of several universities that had the same practices, however, NYU was chosen because it had no policies.8 Software checkout has many aspects and pitfalls until proper acquisition and usage policies can be devised. Librarians must use software and advise producers of their needs.

REFERENCES

1. See Chapter One, "Copyright Basics" of Commonsense Copyright: A Guide to the New Technologies, R. S. Talab, Jefferson, North Carolina, 1986, for an explanation of the application of common law to copyright.

2. Chapman, Christopher. Untangling the copyright issues. Electronic Learning, Nov/Dec., 1985, pp. 43+.

3. P.L. 96-517

4. Latman, A., R. Gorman and J. Ginsburg. Copyright in the Eighties. Charlottesville, VA: The Michie Company, 1985, pp. 513-514.

5. Newsline. Classroom Computer Learning, October, 1985, p. 14.

6. Latman, Gorman and Ginsburg, op. cit., p. 134.

7. ibid., p. 134.

8. Personal communication of Carol Risher of American Publisher's Association to the author, May, 1983.

MACINTOSH DATABASE MANAGEMENT

Janet Vratny-Watts, Apple Computer, Inc.

The excellent user-interface and power features of the Apple
Macintosh have been recognized for the level of quality they bring
to areas like Desktop Publishing, Computer Graphics and Word
Processing.   Imagine the same Macintosh features in other library
applications, like online searching or database management. The
same great mouse-activated icons, pull-down menus and dialog boxes
help to make your database applications more full-featured and
simple to use. In many cases, extensive training of staff and
patrons is not as necessary with Macintosh-based software
applications. Currently, there are many different *Data Base
Management Software (DBMS)* packages on the market for the
Macintosh. In this paper, I will attempt to cover as many of
those as possible in the time permitting.

First, there are simple *File Managers* for the Macintosh. They
are *Heirarchical* in nature, which means that information is stored
in a long list, usually with one indexed field. These basic *DBMS*
software packages are excellent for managing simple, single files
of information, like newsletter mailing lists, periodical
holdings, or simple acquisitions files. You will be pleasantly
surprised to find how easy the Macintosh makes database design and
operation.

Old favorites like *PFS:File* and *DBMaster* are now available on
the Macintosh. While still fairly limited, these programs take on
new qualities when enhanced by Macintosh features, such as easy
form design and command selection via pull-down menus. One of the
best and most popular Macintosh *File Managers* is *Microsoft File*.
Microsoft File features custom or default form design; date format
presets; and unlimited field length. *Microsoft File's* easy
features and qualities make it an excellent library database tool.

If you need to share information between files, or want more
features and power, then *Relational DBMS* software is the answer.
A *Relational DBMS* gives you the ability to take two different
files of information and link them. For example, you might want to
link your acquisitions file to your catalog, so that new book
information would not have to be retyped! Another possibility is
a link or connection between your catalog and patron files, to
simplify circulation. An often added bonus from using *Relational
DBMS* software is flexible and powerful generation of reports and
statistics. There are many excellent *Relational DBMS* packages for
the Macintosh. Choosing one from another will depend upon your
library's needs vs the time you wish to spend setting up your
application.

For example, designing your database application using
Interlace (now known as *Reflex for the Macintosh*) is very simple.
Reflex allows graphic design of complex databases and time-saving
default data entry forms or custom data entry form design with
graphics. *Reflex* is very powerful and fast to use, because it
loads as much of your data into temporary *RAM* (*Random Access
Memory*) memory as possible. This means that the software does not
need to access the disk drive as frequently, making the retrieval

of data much faster. *Reflex* could easily be used to design a database for patron, catalog and circulation information in a small to meduim size library.

OverVUE 2.0 has been ranked as one of the best Macintosh *Relational DBMS* packages on the market. *OverVUE 2.0* is similar to *Reflex* in its spreadsheet-like display of multiple records, and the use of *RAM* for manipulating data. (But it limits the size of the database to the amount of available *RAM*). *OverVUE* provides strong math features; no field length limits; default report formats; default multiple record displays; customizable single record displays; and fast switching from multiple to single record formats. When in the multiple record format, *OverVUE* will try to guess the entire text for a field if the first three letters match the previous record's matching field. *OverVUE* has been easily used for Acquisitions and Interlibrary Loans databases, and is a popular database choice.

Helix 2.0 features unlimited field lengths, that will hold text or graphics. This makes it ideal for databases that include large abstracts, or graphic pictures (like portraits). Applications are designed on *Helix* using Macintosh icons that represent entry layout, file relationships, calculations, etc. This makes *Helix* very different from most other *Relational DBMS* packages for the Macintosh. *Double Helix* was introduced in late 1986, and was Odesta's first offering of *Multi-user* software. This means that a *Double Helix* application could be used by different staff members or patrons at the same time, from different Macintosh installations in your library.

At this current point in time, *OMNIS 3* still seems to be the most powerful *Relational DBMS* application tool for the Macintosh. *OMNIS 3* for the Macintosh has offered multi-user features and completely customizable menus, data entry and report formats for a couple of years now. It is possible to design a completely *Turnkey* application for your library using *OMNIS 3* or *OMNIS 3 Plus*. *Turnkey* means that anyone can use the finished system with no prior knowledge of OMNIS 3. For example, all they might need to know is whether they want to look for something by author, title or subject, and the custom *Turnkey DBMS* will do the rest. *OMNIS 3* and *OMNIS 3 Plus* are not as easy to use as *Microsoft File* or *Reflex*. However, compared to other powerful *DBMS* tools like *Dbase II*, *Dbase III*, etc., the *OMNIS 3 DBMS* products seem to do half your design work for you!

There are a number of other Macintosh *DBMS* packages on the market that were not covered in this presentation due to time constraints. Many of the ones mentioned here have been popular for some time, and hold an excellent reputation. It is important to first decide what your library's database needs are, and how you plan to meet those needs with *DBMS* Software. These decisions are your most important, since they will determine what type of software package you need, and what features you need most. A comparison and choice can then be made that will work best in your library setting.

(Bibliography and Graphics distributed in session.)

SPACE PLANNING AND COLLECTION ANALYSIS WITH ENABLE

Steven G. Watkins, University of California at Santa Cruz

Space problems are not new to libraries. With publishing output undiminished, collections grow at a rate that ensures the eventual inadequacy of available shelf space. New building construction can often be justified only after space constraints have reached crisis proportions. Faced with a facility where the collection has outgrown shelving capacity, library planners must be able to allocate existing space to allow for variable rates of growth, decide which portions of the collection are most appropriate to be moved out of the building to accommodate new materials, and project collection space requirements for a new building.

Library collections are dynamic by their very nature: new materials are added continually; superseded or less-used materials are withdrawn; a certain percentage of the collection is in circulation at any given time; categories of materials grow at different rates and receive varying degrees of use; certain subject areas have larger user constituencies than others. Effective planning is dependent on the availability of accurate, up-to-date data on the size, use and growth of the various components of the collection. Each level of decision making relies on much the same data, although the presentation of the information will vary according to its intended use. Spreadsheets are well suited to the storage and analysis of such highly variable data, particularly when projections and models of variant scenarios are to be based on the data.

Enable, an integrated software program, was purchased with the support of a grant from the Librarians Association of the University of California and used to develop a set of interrelated spreadsheets that model the science collection at UC Santa Cruz. The building can accommodate only half of the 190,000 volume collection; the remainder is shelved across campus in the main library. There is substantial pressure from the academic departments to maintain equitable distribution of the resources housed at the Science Library. Since 10,000 volumes are added each year, a comparable number must be moved out of the building each summer. The process of selecting materials to be moved attempts to keep the most used and most relevant titles at the Science Library until a new building is constructed.

First, to provide a rationale for the library's selections in discussions with the faculty, several spreadsheets were developed to map those portions of the collection related by subject to each academic department, calculate what percentage of each department's collection is housed in each of the two libraries, and correlate circulation statistics with the size of the user population from each depart-

ment. These figures provide a quantitative picture of the
size and relative use of each subject collection, information that can be used in conjunction with the staff's judg-
ment to decide which portions of the collection to move.

A second set of spreadsheets is used to allocate shelf
space to the remaining collection, allowing for variable
rates of growth among the different call number ranges.
Each floor of the building is mapped on a spreadsheet,
indicating by LC class number the size of the collection,
the amount of material to be moved out, and the number of
volumes added annually. The size of the collection after
one year's growth is projected for each classification and
the linear shelf space needed to house it is calculated.
The vertical dimension of the stacks is brought into the
equation by calculating the average number of shelves that
can be fit into each section of shelving. The resulting
figures make it possible to allocate to each classification
the requisite number of sections of shelving and determine
how many inches of books to put on each shelf to allow for
growth. The existing collection, minus the material to be
moved, is then spread out into the available space. The
ability to use windows to move data between spreadsheets
with Enable allows one to experiment with alternate configurations of the collection in the building, such as moving
call number ranges from one floor to another.

Detailed planning for the construction of a new science
library has recently begun. Data compiled for coping with
the existing building formed the basis of a spreadsheet for
projecting twenty-year space requirements. Different growth
rates for each five-year period may be entered to reflect
campus plans for new academic programs in upcoming years.
Assignable square feet for the life science and physical
science collections was calculated using library space planning standards. Using Enable's integrated features, a
summary chart from the spreadsheet was inserted directly
into the word processing text of the building proposal.
When preliminary drawings are received from the architects,
the proposed layout of the collection can be revised if
necessary to fit design constraints.

The present system provides management information to
the library's professional staff to assist in decision
making, computes detailed figures that enable the stack
supervisor to carry out those decisions, and produces
summary information for campus facility planners and state
budget officials. It has potential additional applications
in the allocation of the library materials budget and the
weeding of the collection.

Enable(TM) is a trademark of The Software Group.

153

IDENTIFYING THE PROBLEM

SESSION NINETEEN: Getting the System Up and Running
Part II - Managing the Microcomputer Automation Project

by Maggie Weaver

Successful implementation of computer systems is more than just
selecting the right software and hardware and learning to use them.
It involves management: analysis, strategies, planning, contracts,
people, training, marketing. This is true whether you are automating
circulation in a public library, or your budget in a one-person
corporate information centre.

Your initial needs analysis should cover not only system specifications,
but also management requirements. Do I need technical support to
install or run the system? Will I need clerical help during conversion
or afterwards? How will I sell the system to management? Will existing
workflows be affected by the new procedure? These questions will
stimulate some more fundamental ones: am I tackling the real problem, is
automation the real solution, do I have the necessary time and skills?

Often, you will need help with management issues, just as you need it
with technical ones. Objective, experienced outsiders can help you
identify problems, assess alternative solutions, estimate time demands,
evaluate skills, "sell" the system to management and users, get you
and your staff adjusted to new work patterns.

The three speakers have addressed these management issues as external
consultant, internal consultant, and client. Their library experience
is varied, but their message is the same: success depends on effective
management as well as appropriate technology.

154

DEVELOPING A STATEWIDE COMMUNITY RESOURCE DATABASE:
THE INDIANA YOUTH RESOURCES INFORMATION NETWORK

Becki Whitaker
Indiana Cooperative Library Services Authority

The Indiana Youth Resources Information Network (IYRIN)
is a project of the Indiana Cooperative Library Services
Authority (INCOLSA) and 15 public libraries in Indiana which
have jointly developed a statewide database for community
resources. The database includes information about
agencies and organizations in Indiana which provide services
to their communities. Initial funding for the project was a
grant from the Indiana Criminal Justice Institute in July
1985. The first version of the statewide database was
available in June, 1986. The entire database is updated
every six months. The IYRIN database is mounted on a
decentralized local area network (LAN). The network design
and software development will be discussed by Mr. Jay Hayden
in his presentation.

Medium-sized public libraries in Indiana were invited
to apply for participation in the project. Criteria for
selection of participants included geographic distribution,
size of library, and willingness to commit to the project.
All 15 libraries which did apply were included in the
project. Grant funds supported the initial purchase of
equipment, software and consulting. Additional funds for
equipment support and staffing were committed by INCOLSA and
each library. The project has no full time staff. Existing
INCOLSA and library staff have assumed the extra workload.

An independent consultant was hired to make
recommendations about software selection, the content and
design of the record, and vocabulary control for subject
searching. Price, record structure, built-in capabilities
of the software package plus ease of local modification were
major considerations for software selection. DBase III was
selected.

Standardization of the record format was of utmost
importance in the record design. It was also desired that
the record structure also needed to be comprehensive,
transportable, expandable, functional, and flexible.
Participating libraries aided the consultant in record

155

design. The record contains 31 fields; 17 of which are
mandatory for every record. An IYRIN Questionnaire,
Indexer's Instructions, and an Input Form help ensure
standardization.

The consultant also made recommendations regarding a
controlled vocabulary. The final selection of the Thesaurus
of ERIC Descriptors as the vocabulary authority was made by
the INCOLSA IYRIN staff in consultation with the
participating libraries. Controlled vocabularies for
geographic searching were also designed, enabling searching
from the zip code level to the statewide and national
levels.

Since most of the library staff members came to the
project with no microcomputer experience, a comprehensive,
structured training program was mandated. Each library
designated an IYRIN contact person and back-up. These
people were required to attend six training sessions during
the period December 1985 through September 1986. The
sessions dealt with equipment operation, software, indexing
techniques, and discussions on systems design and policies.
Additional sessions and alternative training methods are
planned. The IYRIN contact people are responsible for
additional in-house staff and user training with the
assistance of INCOLSA staff.

The 15 libraries have made local decisions about output
formats and access modes based on the options provided by
the IYRIN software. The search software is menu driven and
can be used with some instruction by end users. Each
library will determine whether or not end users will search.

The management of a decentralized network has required
a mechanism to ensure input from all participants and allow
equal representation in the decision making process.
Therefore, a Quality Control Committee which is responsible
for monitoring any apparent problems with quality,
standardization, or conflicts in policy development has been
established.

MICROAIDE, A MICROCOMPUTER USERS' NETWORK

Frank White, Department of Finance/Treasury Board of Canada

MICROAIDE is a microcomputer users' network for federal government libraries in Canada to facilitate the free exchange of information and knowledge relating to the use of microcomputers in libraries.

Few would disagree that learning how to use microcomputers productively can be time consuming and frustrating. Our library acquired its first microcomputer in July 1985, and it quickly became apparent that information sharing among a network of users could accelerate the learning process and improve the quality of decision making.

So how does one go about establishing a microcomputer users' network?

I began by doing what any good bureaucrat would do - I tried to get somebody else to do the work. I took my idea to the Chairman of the Priority and Planning Committee of the Council of Federal Libraries. The Chairman, no bureaucratic slouch himself, threw the proposal right back in my lap, suggesting that I take it on as a project.

As the project leader the first task I set myself was to measure the support in the Canadian federal government library community for the establishment of a microcomputer users' network. In January of 1986 I sent out a brief questionnaire to about 150 federal government libraries located in the region of our national capital. On the basis of the enthusiastic support for the network, I decided to proceed.

In April of 1986, I met with a group of about ten other librarians who had indicated a willingness to assist in getting the network up and running. This group, an official task group of the Council of Federal Libraries, met once a month throughout the remainder of 1986, making these significant decisions:
1. The users' network would be called MICROAIDE, a name which serves the bilingual nature of our community of prospective users.
2. Invitations to join MICROAIDE, accompanied by application forms, would be sent to all (about 320) federal government library locations in Canada, including branch and regional offices of headquarters' libraries.

1

3. Membership would be restricted to the Canadian federal library community.

4. An indexed directory of users' hardware and software resources would be produced and distributed to facilitate information sharing among members. The application form would be used to gather this information.

5. Edibase, a text-based management system developed and distributed by INFORM II of Montreal, would be used to produce the bilingual directory.

6. Members would be requested to renew their membership annually and to update their directory information at the same time.

7. Suggestions to provide an electronic bulletin board and a newsletter to supplement the directory were rejected; however, we did agree to review these decisions in a year.

8. There will be an evaluation of network use in 1987, one result of which will be the identification of other ways to serve members.

In August of 1986, invitations, accompanied by application forms, were sent to all federal government libraries. By the November 15th deadline, 98 libraries had joined the network, including the National Library of Canada, the Canadian Institute for Scientific & Technical Information and those of most other major federal government departments.

The Directory has been produced and has been sent to the Council of Federal Libraries for printing and distribution to members.

A cursory glance through the Directory and its many indexes reveals three not surprising discoveries about microcomputer applications in Canadian federal government libraries:

1. IBM and IBM compatibles dominate in terms of hardware;

2. dBASE III, Lotus 1-2-3, Crosstalk XVI, and Word Perfect are some of the software winners; and

3. generally speaking, the bigger the library the more resources, with many smaller libraries still waiting to acquire their first microcomputer.

The choice of software to produce the directory was based on a comparison of Edibase with dBASE III Plus to produce a prototype directory. As a text-based management system, Edibase is designed for just this type of application, and given its bilingual capability, it proved superior to dBASE III in terms of ease of use and quality of results achieved in the shortest period of time.

2

THE ONLINE LIBRARIAN'S MICROCOMPUTER USER GROUP: TELECONFERENCING BY AND FOR LIBRARIANS

Brian Williams
California Polytechnic State University, SLO

The Online Librarian's Microcomputer User Group, OLMUG, is a teleconferencing system for librarians working with microcomputers. The purpose of the service is mutual support of library microcomputer applications. It is a natural application for teleconferencing, for three reasons:

1.   Library applications of microcomputers are somewhat specialized and justify their own user group, but those involved in the applications are too widely spread apart to attend conventional user group meetings, for the most part.

2.   Microcomputer problems frequently require person to person communication to solve. It is very hard to find answers in the literature and manuals are usually deficient. Usually one tries to find an expert to ask questions of by phone.

3.   At the same time, those in libraries using microcomputers are more likely to have a basic familiarity with the communications technology used in teleconferencing, which can be a stumbling block otherwise.

Teleconferencing substitutes for some kinds of meetings. It does not provide the full range of communication that a face to face meeting does, but it does not require individuals to drive long distances to make their contributions either. In addition, meetings are asynchronous; participants are not required to be involved at the same time of day or even the same time of the week, so that communication takes place at the convenience of the schedule of the participant and can be incorporated smoothly into the organized daily work flow. A hard copy record of what transpires is a natural outcome of the teleconferencing meeting.

OLMUG uses the Confer II software running on Wayne State University's computer. This environment meets several

159

of the prerequisites for such a system as OLMUG.

1. It has nationwide access via a major data network,
    Telenet, in this case.

2. Wayne State will allow organizations from outside
    its own institution to set up accounts and use
    their computer facilities.

3. They have excellent teleconferencing software
    running on their equipment.

4. Their costs are competitive.

Confer II was written by Bob Parnes of Advertel for IBM
mainframes running the Michigan Terminal System (MTS)
operating system. It is a command driven system with lots of
online help and good manuals. Its features include a good
electronic mail system and automatic notification of all new
material. Additions to the existing items and the addition
of new items is easy. There is a bulletin feature which
automatically sends messages to all the participants once
when they log on, and participants can engage in real time
conversations, if they desire. Most of the conversations are
asynchronous, with participants adding input at their
convenience. There is a line editor online, and several file
management capabilities.

As the Robert E. Kennedy Library at California
Polytechnic State University, San Luis Obispo, is sponsoring
this system and subsidizing the work of organizing and
managing it, there is no sign up charge, or monthly fee.
participants pay only for time spent online. The access
rates are $17 per hour during prime time, 7AM - 7PM Eastern
Standard Time Monday through Friday, and $10 per hour at all
other times. Users are billed by Kennedy Library. The
benefits to participants include support with microcomputer
projects, cooperative assessment of software, ongoing
discussions of microcomputer applications in libraries, and
access to the accumulated knowledge of all the participants.
There is no limit to the number of participants or the
amount of material that can be available online.

Accounts on OLMUG are available from Brian Williams,
Robert E. Kennedy Library, Cal Poly, San Luis Obispo, Ca. 93407.

BUILD YOURSELF A GENERIC COMPUTER

Mark Wilson
Assistant Dean for Learning Resources
Juniata College

No, "Generic Computer" is not the punch line of a joke. A generic computer is one composed of standard and interchangable parts based on the IBM XT. A generic computer may be built by anyone who can handle a screwdriver. But the best news is that a generic computer costs less than $700.

This article describes step-by-step how to obtain the parts necessary to build a generic computer and how to assemble them into a working computer. No electronic or soldering skills are needed; if you can use a screwdriver and are willing to follow all of the instructions, you should be able to build your own IBM XT clone in about two hours.

Ordering the Parts

The simplest method, but not the most economical, is to purchase all parts from a single dealer. In any event, review the advertisements in *The Computer Shopper* available at most magazine stands (ISSN 0886-0556, 407 S. Washington Avenue, Titusville, FL 32781) and order these parts:

$150	(1) motherboard with BIOS and 640K RAM *installed*
60	(1) monochrome graphics adapter with printer port.
26	(1) floppy disk adapter (two drive version)
45	(1) 150 watt power supply
27	(1) XT type slide-in comptuer case
80	(1) TTL monochrome monitor (amber or green)
45	(1) XT/AT style keyboard
80(each)	(2) 360K double sided double density drive
50-80	(1) *MS-DOS* with *GW BASIC* (version 3.1 or 3.2)

The above prices may vary slightly from dealer to dealer. Not every dealer will have all of the components. The prices quoted are from Rigid Merchandise (800-843-9134) for mother-board, monochrome and disk adapters, power supply, case and keyboard; from American Semiconductor (800-247-2271) for the disk drives; from Magitronic Technology (800-227-5454) for the monitor; and Sunnytech, Inc. (800-367-1132) for the *MS-DOS* with *GW BASIC*. Citation of a particular dealer does not imply endorsement; the information is given simply to indicate that the best total price will more than likely come by dealing with several vendors.

The dealers listed in *The Computer Shopper* should provide satisfaction. Buyers are cautioned to purcahse the motherboard with the BIOS chip and 640K RAM *already installed*, and to ensure that the *MS-DOS* price includes *GW BASIC* and manuals. You may wish to ask about return policies, guarantees, and technical assistance. As with any mail-order, do-it-yourself project, some risk is incurred.

No Experience Needed

The following instruction have been used successfully by two Penn State University librarians (both claimed no mechanical experience to assemble a generic computer). They report that the most difficult task was learning the names of the parts. Therefore, readers with limited mechanical experience might want to separate the hardware parts shipped with the computer case and carefully compare them to the drawings (Figure 1).

One of the best ways to do so involves an ordinary kitchen muffin pan. As small bits of hardware are found, place each in a different compartment in the muffin pan with an identifying label.

Read completely through each section before attempting to do the assembly described. Handle all of the parts carefully and tighten screws gently. Try to hold the boards by their edges and avoid touching "golden finger" plugs on each board.

And, before beginning, go to your local hardware store and purchase eight #6 half-inch round-headed screws to be used in mounting the disk drives. Most cases are shipped with screws too short to do the job.

The Computer Case

The case consists of three components: the chassis, the cover, and a box of hardware. Manufacturers typically tuck the box of hardware inside an already assembled case. Figure 1 describes the hardware, Figure 4 describes the front and back of the chassis. Begin by locating and removing the five screws on the rear panel (Figure 4) that fasten the cover to the chassis. Remove the cover by sliding it forward, then put the cover aside. Open the hardware box and separate the components. The box should contain the following:

    four rubber feet
    six silver rear slot covers
    six black front slot mounts
    two (frequently only one) black rear panel covers
    one metal disk drive rack
    seven plastic standoffs
    one brass hex standoff and hex nut
    one large self-tapping screw
    two fiber washers
    several small screws (number varies)
    several hex screws (number varies)

Refer to Figure 1 for outline drawings of the hardware pack contents.

The first step is to place the rubber feet at the four corners of the underside of the chassis. Turn the chassis upside-down on the worktable, remove the paper backing from one rubber foot, and use its self-adhesive backing to attach it to the chassis an inch or two from the corner. Repeat until a foot has been placed at each corner, but be careful not to cover any screws or holes with the feet.

Return the chassis to an upright position. Refer to Figure 3 and examine the inside of the front panel. On the left side of the front panel is a speaker cage. On the rear of the speaker cage and directly across from the eight slots on the back panel are two rows of six holes each, one row at the top of the cage, one row near the bottom.

Take the six black front slot mounts (Figure 1) from the hardware package and observe that one side of each is slotted, the other side has two tabs. Fasten the six front slot mounts vertically to the rear of the speaker cage by pushing the two tabs into two of the holes.

The chassis is now ready to receive the remaining sub-assemblies: the motherboard, the power supply, the disk drives, and the adapter boards. Be very careful to keep in mind the orientation of the chassis as the parts are mounted.

The Motherboard

Take the motherboard from its box and compare it to Figure 2. Note that the motherboard (any any circuit board) has two sides: the component side (with all the parts) and the solder side (with the prickly pins sticking out). Referring to Figures 1 and 2, locate the plastic standoffs and insert these through the proper holes in the motherbaord. Note that each standoff is shaped like an arrowhead and is poked through the holes from the solder side to the component side.

Next, locate the hex standoff and the hex nut. Again, push the threaded part of the hex standoff through the proper hole from the solder side of the board and gently fasten it to the board with the nut. The nut will be on the component side, the hex portion of the standoff on the solder side of the motherboard.

Finally, locate the switch pack with eight switches on the motherboard (see Figure 2). Note on the switch the tiny word "ON". Moving one of the switches in that direction will turn it on; moving it in the oppostie direction turns it off. All eight switches need to be set properly. Switch 1 should always be set to off.

The remaining switches are used to tell the computer about extra equipment. Here it is assumed that a co-processor (called a 8087 chip at a cost of about $130) has not been installed, that 640K of RAM have been installed, that two disk drives are being installed, and that a monochrome board will be installed.

ANY VARIATION FROM THIS CONFIGURATION WILL REQUIRE DIFFERENT SWITCH SETTINGS. Read the manual accompanying the motherboard to determine alternate switch settings or call your dealer.

Set switches 2 through 8 as follows:

Switch 2   ON (no co-processor)
Switch 3 & 4 OFF (full memory installed)
Switch 5 & 6 OFF (monochrome adapter installed)

163

Switch 7   OFF (two disk drives installed)
Switch 8   ON (two disk drives installed)

The motherboard is now fully assembled and ready for mounting in the chassis. It is very important to note that the slots in the motherbaord will be near the rear of the chassis and that the memory block will end up near the front.

Assembling the Computer

Hint: Examine Figures 2 and 3 VERY carefully. Read through these instructions before actually doing the assembly.

Place the chassis on the worktable and note the keyhold-like holes in the three rails fastened to the floor of the chassis (Figure 3). The bottom flanges of the plastic standoffs must each fit in these keyholes. Orient the chassis to a comfortable working position, and with the component side up, gently, gently fit the motherboard to the rails.

Note that the motherboard slots are near the rear of the chassis and the memory to the front (refer to Figure 1). Note also that the rear rail has only two keyholes; the third position is a small hole in the floor of the case. The bottom of the hex standoff will be positioned directly above that hole and one of the smallest screws from the hardware set will be used to hold it in place.

Observe that the front rail also has only two keyholes. Once the motherboard is in place, locate the two fiber insulators and sheet metal screw. Slide on insulator between the underside of the board and the screw bracket in the rail, center the other over the hole on top of the motherboard, and gently tighten the self-tapping screw. The fiber insulators should keep the screw and its underside bracket from touching the motherboard.

Good luck with this step as it is the most difficult to perform in the entire assembly. An alternative is to lightly glue the fiber washers to the motherboard, one above and one below the center front hole.) Don't forget to fasten the hex standoff through the floor of the chassis with one of the small screws. Now locate the small wire and plug coming from the speaker. Refer to Figure 2 and plug this wire to the motherboard speaker plug.

The Power Supply

The power supply is the heavy metal box with fan holes and wires coming out of it. Examine it closely. Its rear panel is the side with the two electrical outlet plug (one male, one female). There should be four screw holes, one in each corner of the rear panel of the power supply. Sometimes there are screws mounted in these four holes. If there are, remove them.

Look at the underside of the power supply. Now look at the rear right hand side of the chassis and note the two tabs rising from the floor. Gently fasten the power supply to the chassis by sliding the tabs into the slots (remember the power outlets face the rear of the chassis and the on/off switch sticks out the right hand side).

Once the tabs and slots are engaged, slide the power supply back against the rear plate of the chassis and fasten it ot the rear plate with the four screws removed earlier. (Note variation: some power supplies come with the four screws removed but in a plastic bag, some require the use of the four largest screws in the hardware box.)

Now examine the six clusters of wires that come out of the left side of the power supply. Four of them are twins, each consisting of four wires and identical plugs. Ignore the four twins and carefully examine the two remaining bundles of wire. One is made up of six wires, the other of five.

Look carefully at the plug containing six wires. Three of them are read. Refer to Figure 2 and locate the power plug on the motherboard. Orient the six-wire plug so that the three red wires are closest to the front of the motherboard and very carefully mount it vertically (it will snap firmly in place) on the power plug on the motherboard.

DOUBLE CHECK THESE INSTRUCTIONS as a mistake could destroy tne motherboard. If the bundle has been properly plugged to the motherboard there should be six empty spikes sticking out of the rear part of the plug on the motherboard.

Now take the plug containing the five wires. Note that one side of the plug has six tiny teeth while the other side has one long tab. Observe that the six wire plug already mounted to the board has the same design. When plugging these bundles of wire to the motherboard, the six tiny teeth go on the motherboard side, the long tab goes on the power supply side. Double check and insert the five wire plug into the rearmost part of the motherboard plug. Both plugs from the power supply should fit snugly up against each other. Check and recheck that the plugs are in the right sequence (six-wire to the front, five-wire to the back), and that all of the spikes in the motherplug are fitted into the power supply plugs.

The Disk Drives

These instructions presume two half-height 360K floppy disk drives and will not work for other devices. Be sure to seek competent help if you have elected another configuration. Please note that while the disk drive installation instructions appear long and complex, the process is rather simple.

Unpack the two drives but leave the cardboard insert inside the disk drive to protect its heads from damage. Near the rear of the drive will be a set of eight pins arranged in two rows of four pins each (labeled DS0, DS1, DS2, DS3) sticking up from the component side of its circuit board. One set of pins should have a small black device, called a jumper, plugged over them. If the jumper is covering the pins marked DS1, leave it there, If not, gently pull the jumper from its present position and place it over the DS1 pins.

Now carefully examine the components on the disk drive's circuit board. Note all of the long black catepillar like objects; these are computer chips (Figure 5). Most should be soldered directly to the circuit board but one or more will be raised above the board by sockets. Look closely at any chips in sockets (ignore those soldered directly to the circuit board). On the circuit board near each will be some writing.

Locate the chip in a socket labeled 'RN1' (sometimes only 'RN'). It should be quite close to the jumpered pins dealth with earlier. Being very careful not to injure the circuit board, gently remove the chip labeled 'RN1' from its socket, but do this only to one of the drives. Removing this chip turns the drive into what will be called a B drive; leaving the chip in place turns it into what will be called an A drive. Each computer will need both an A drive and a B drive.

Ensure that the jumper is over the DS1 pins on both drives and that one drive is an A drive (computer chip RN1 in place) and that one drive is a B drive (computer chip RN1 removed). The drives are now ready for mounting.

165

Carefully examine the drive to determine which side is the top, which the bottom. Since various manufacturers build their drives differently, the orientation of each drive may vary. However, the 'bottom' of the drive will be the side that seems naturally the bottom.

On the drives in hand, the circuit board is the top, the belt-drive on the bottom. Assume the lumpy side is the top, the smooth side the bottom.

There are two large slots on the front panel of the chassis (Figure 4). Take the B drive (computer chip RN1 removed) and slip it carefully into the right hand slot. Sometimes the fit may be snug: be very gentle, but firm, and be very careful not to damage any of the components on the top or bottom of the drive.

Turn the chassis and observe the drive rail on the side of the chassis; it will be next to the drive and contains eight oval-shaped screw holes. Through the bottom-most holes, threaded holes in the disk drive chassis should be visible.

There should have been some quarter-inch hex screws in the chassis hardware package. While these screws were meant to mount the drive, most often they are too short. If you have not made the trip to the hardware store suggested earlier, now is the time. Take one of these hex-headed screws to a hardware store and get eight longer screws with a similar thread.

Attach the B drive to the rail with two of these screws, then attach the removable disk drive mounting rack (Figure 1) to the other side of the disk drive, again with two screws. Note that the tab on the mounting rack faces front and down. The B drive is now fully mounted.

Take any one of the four bundles of wire coming out of the power supply. Examine the male plug at the end of the wire and look for a similar female plug on the disk drive. The plug may only be inserted in one position, so if it refuses to plug into the disk drive, turn the plug over and try again.

Finally, mount the A drive above the B drive in the same slot. Follow the directions given in the instructions for the B drive. The front panel of the drives should be flush against the front panel of the computer chassis.

Be sure to note which drive is which. The A drive is in the top position and the B drive in the bottom position.

Mounting the Adapter Boards

The adapter boards plug into the motherboard's slots. There are four things to keep in mind as the adapter boards are plugged in:

1. The boards will run from front to rear;
2. The component sides face the power supply;
3. The boards mount at 90-degree angles;
4. The 'gold fingers' plug into the motherboard slots.

Locate the monochrome adapter oard and the disk adapter board. Orient the monochrome board so that the golden plug is at the bottom, ready to slip into the leftmost slot on the motherboard. Carefully plug it into the motherboard slot, but make sure the front of the board is in the leftmost black slot on the rear of the speaker cage, that the silver end slips into the slot at the rear of the chassis, and that the golden fingers skip into the slot on the rear of the motherboard. Fasten the top of the silver connector to the slot mount at the rear of the chassis with one of the smaller screws.

The disk adapter board comes in two sizes, long or short. The short disk adapter board may be fitted into any of the remaining slots on the motherboard, but the long disk adapter board will fit only those slots behind the speaker cage. Mount the disk adapter board in a manner similar to the monochrome adapter board.

Observe the cable that came with the disk adapter board (Figure 4). At one end the middle of the cable is twisted just before it enters the plug. That plug, when properly oriented, will be inserted into the A drive. The middle plug must be attached to the B drive, and the plug at the end oposite the twist attaches to the adapter board.

Look inside the plug with the twist in the cable; close to one end of the slot should be a small bar blocking the entrance to the plug hole. Also, the cable itself should have one colored wire on the same side as the blocking bar. Now look at the golden fingers plug at the rear of one of the disk drive; note the small slit at one end of the disk drive plug. The bar and colored wire must be placed at that end of the plug.

Take the middle plug in the cable and orient it so that the colored wire and blocking bar match the slit in the golden plug on the B drive. Then carefully plug the cable to the B drive board. Take the plug with the twisted cable and attach it in the same manner to the A drive board.

Now examine the disk adapter board. If it is the short type, there is a golden plug at the front of the board. Plug the end of the disk cable, with the colored wire up, to this plug. The long boards use a double pin arrangement in a horizontal position. Plug the cable to tha board with the color strip facing the front of the computer. On the long disk adapter boards the proper socket is labeled "Disk" and is at the front and top of the board.

Finishing Up

The computer can now be operated, but some small details need to be taken care of. First, cover the empty front hole with the two plastic bezels. Next, fill in the empty rear slots with the silver slot covers and the black rear slot cover (use small screws). Then slip the cover over the chassis and fasten it with the screws removed earlier.

The monitor cable plugs into the small plug at the top of the monochrome adapter (the top leftmost plug on the rear; the bottom leftmost plug is for a parallel printer). Plug the monitor power plug into the wall. Plug the keyboard into its socket at the rear of the computer. Now take the cord that came with the power supply and plug it into the outlet on the rear of the comptuer; plug the other end into the wall. The computer is now ready to be turned on.

First remove the cardboard inserts from the drive, then put a *DOS* disk into drive A and close the drive handle. Then turn on the monitor and finally turn on the switch on the side of the computer.

Happy computing!

167

FIGURE 1. Hardware. (Note: figures are not drawn to scale)

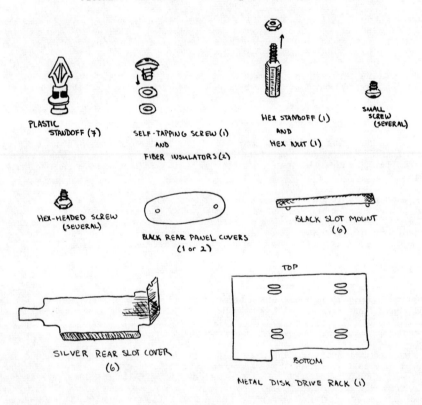

PLASTIC STANDOFF (7)

SELF-TAPPING SCREW (1)
AND
FIBER INSULATORS (2)

HEX STANDOFF (1)
AND
HEX NUT (1)

SMALL SCREW (SEVERAL)

HEX-HEADED SCREW (SEVERAL)

BLACK REAR PANEL COVERS (1 or 2)

BLACK SLOT MOUNT (6)

SILVER REAR SLOT COVER (6)

TOP

BOTTOM

METAL DISK DRIVE RACK (1)

FIGURE 2. The Mother Board

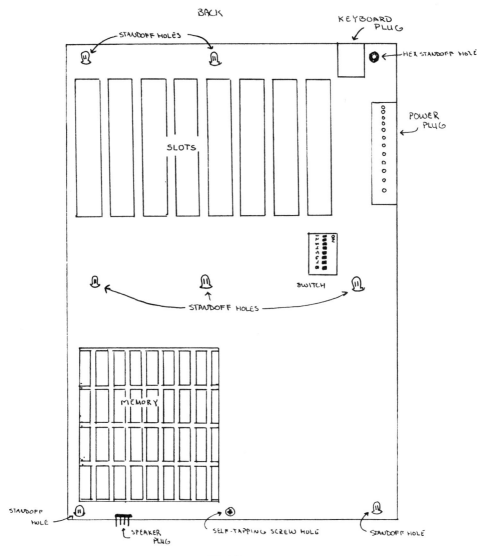

FIGURE 3 Top view of chassis floor.

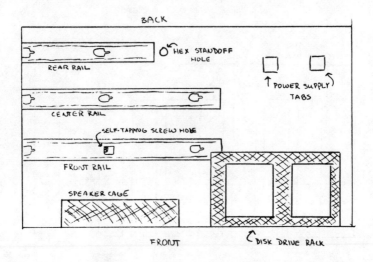

BACK

HEX STANDOFF HOLE

REAR RAIL

POWER SUPPLY TABS

CENTER RAIL

SELF-TAPPING SCREW HOLE

FRONT RAIL

SPEAKER CAGE

FRONT

DISK DRIVE RACK

170

FIGURE 4   Chassis front and back and disk drive cable

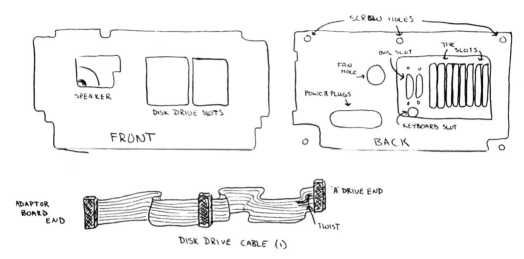

FIGURE 5. Computer chip.

Addendum

The Library's Microcomputer Laboratory:
The Seed of New Technology

Lisa A. Camardo
Coordinator, Computer Support Services
Raymond Walters College
University of Cincinnati

We, who are microcomputer lab managers, are much like first time parents who have had no prior experience with raising and caring for a child. From the day a newborn is brought home, the parents need to learn how to provide for its needs. They can read books or talk to others who have more experience but many new parents simply learn by trial and error. The overall greatest concern in rearing a child is helping that child to grow and prosper to the best of its ability within its environment. In much the same way, the microcomputer lab manager shares many of the responsibilities as new parents, and the lab goes through stages of development. Our experience followed this sequence of events:

1. Birth
2. Needs Assessment - Follow-Up
3. Evaluating/Purchasing
4. Training
5. Scheduling
6. Next Generation

BIRTH

When the new computer arrives at your site, it needs to be assembled and configured to fit its surroundings. Much like positioning a baby's crib away from drafty windows, the first concern is to keep the computer in a static-free room, away from direct sunlight and in an area which allows access to all sides of the unit. The manager must learn how to feed and clean the computer and determine the cause of problems that arise. Very similar to a child's variation in crying for food or changing, the computer sounds a variety of audible tones and visual error codes on the monitor when it is in need of repair or reconfiguration. A table of these codes and tones can be found in most microcomputer repair books or in the Guide to Operations.

So, we've brought our "baby" home and have provided it with comfortable surroundings. We've learned to determine its "cries" and are prepared to feed and clean our little "bundle of joy." Multiply all this by the number of computer units in your lab (mine is 30) and now we can see the "family" which the microcomputer lab houses.

173

Once the "family" is in place, the lab manager needs to help it to grow and be prosperous. This task in not as easy as you might expect.

The IBM Microcomputer Lab at Raymond Walters College opened in January 1985. Our aim was to offer a resource facility in the form of an open laboratory under the direction of the college library. As part of the library, we could offer free use of the microcomputers and a variety of software applications and hardware configurations to our faculty and students on an equal basis.

The open lab concept had its advantages in the initial stage of the lab's birth. The light usage at that time allowed for some breathing room for trial and error troubleshooting. The easing into a full service laboratory with user support also gave us time to develop a sufficient means of surveying the college as to their expectations of such a facility.

NEEDS ASSESSMENT - FOLLOW-UP

In the needs assessment stage, we sent a questionnaire to each faculty member asking for suggestions of how we might accomodate their classes. We needed to know who was interested in using the lab, what software applications they wanted to teach, and how we could best train them. Most of the respondents expressed great interest but admitted having very little knowledge as to what was available. Some had so little knowledge, they couldn't even suggest ways they might use the lab. Therefore, many of the decisions were placed directly upon the lab manager.

EVALUATING/PURCHASING

The lab manager was to evaluate and purchase software applications which corresponded to the surveyed needs. The lab manager then becomes a consumer and a money manager. It is the duty of the manager to carefully evaluate cleaning products, accessories and compatable software to use with the computer and to purchase these products at a reasonable cost. Carefully reading label descriptions and shopping around for a good price, gives the lab manager a better understanding of the resources available. (Tip: Don't be afraid to negotiate prices with different vendor. Many of them work with elastic price structures.)

When choosing software, there are typically 3 resources to draw from: 1) there are commercially distributed packages, many that offer educational discounted prices or site license agreements; 2) those that are in the public domain, which usually cost only the price of the disk they come on; 3) and the software given to the Library by donation. I chose to purchase word processing software of different levels, accepted some training software and a spreadsheet package as donations to the library collection and also got some public domain programs for database management and telecommunications. With limited software, the lab was operational and training sessions were offered by the lab manager

TRAINING

Shortly after the facility opened, we agreed to choose one word processing package to use as a standard for the college. I began conducting orientation sessions for any classes who wanted to integrate word processing or computer instruction into their curriculum. The orientation sessions usually lasted one hour and covered such basic things as machine operation, disk handling and a beginner's lesson in word processing or other software package relating to their class. We encouraged all departments of the college to participate in the orientation sessions hoping to bring to light the various uses of the computer.

During the summer months workshops were offered for faculty and staff on a number of software applications and began to expand our software collection to more specific needs. For example, some professors had a particular software package at home or in their office that they had been using for some time and wanted to teach their students. They could request that we purchase a copy or multiple copies for use in the lab.

SCHEDULING

As the fall quarter approached, the orientation sessions continued and we continued to encourage the faculty to send students to the lab for homework assignments, special projects and software support. During this quarter, however, many faculty members began to express an interest in conducting their classes in the lab to work on whole group assignments. This caused a problem for those teachers who were sending their students to the lab for "lab" work. The facility became unavailable during those class times and the complaints were strong.

Winter quarter was extremely experimental. We started
scheduling classes into the facility based on written
requests submitted weekly. These scheduled class sessions
were posted outside the lab so that students could make
arrangement to use the lab during "open times". Now we could
start to see a distinct pattern of usage emerge. The lab
was accommodating three levels of users: heavy users, those
classes that used the lab approximately ten hours or more
per quarter; moderate users, those classes that came to the
lab once or twice then sent their students to the lab for
continuing assignments; and the occasional users, those
classes that would come once or twice during the quarter
with one lab assignment.

In order to set a policy for scheduling the lab, we
looked at these levels and focused in on the moderate users.
This middle group, the accounting classes, programming
classes and the online information retrieval classes taught
through the Library Technology Program were scheduling the
lab about five to ten hours per quarter. This seemed to be
a fair amount of time for guided instruction and the
students still returned to the lab outside of class for lab
work. We knew that the heavy users, if given the
opportunity, would schedule the lab for every class meeting
during the quarter. For these people, a little planning
needed to be done before the start of each quarter. The
occasional users could be squeezed in throughout the quarter
because their needs were confined to one assignment.

Prior to spring break, faculty members were sent a grid
of the lab's hours of operation. They were instructed to
write their name in the slot they wished to schedule the lab
and return the grids to me. I arranged them into a master
schedule. All conflicts were resolved based on the total
number of hours requested. Our goal was to accommodate as
many different courses as possible. Therefore, priority was
given to the occasional users. For those classes with less
than fifteen students, the facility could be divided by
temporary partitions, which allowed access to the other
half of the lab for individual users or for another small
class meeting at the same hour.

During this quarter, what began as a resource facility
had become an electronic classroom. There were complaints
from many instructors who regarded the lab as a resource
facility. They were reporting their students' comments that
the lab was too full with classes for them to get in and
complete their homework assignments. Each new complaint
called for immediate remedies which, at times, strayed from
policy.

The decision was made to pull two computers and a
printer out of the lab and make them available in the
Library for those times when classes were being conducted in
the lab. Secondly, a limit was put on the number of hours a
specific course could be taught in the lab facility. That
number directly related to our moderate users who were
scheduled for five to ten hours per quarter. To resolve
conflicts within this new policy, each instructor was asked
to supply on the request form not only the days they
prefered to use the lab but also an alternate date in case
their first choice could not be scheduled. Eventually,
instructors within the same department began to collaborate
with each other about the days and times they scheduled the
lab considerably reducing the number of preliminary
conflicts.

Now that the lab had found its niche in the college, it
began to develop according to its environment. Often,
various departments at the occasional users level such as
Nursing, Dental Hygiene, and Foreign Language, would need
specialized hardware to support simulation programs in their
subject area. So options were added to a small number of
computers now marked "reserved" for these students. The more
specialized the hardware got, the more the lab settled back
into the realm of the original concept; a resource facility.
A natural metamorphisis occurred around this time. The
temporary partition which divided the lab into two
classrooms was now used more often to divide the lab into a
classroom side and a lab side. On the classroom side,
fifteen computers with identical configurations and
peripherals were located as opposed to the specialized
configurations found on the laboratory side.

THE NEXT GENERATION

As the heavy users found a need for even more hands-on
class sessions and the lab was branching out to accommodate
more departments, a natural birthing if you will, occurred.
Smaller labs with specific applications (and a different
personality) were created. The microcomputer lab had grown
up and bore another infant lab. One that needed a manager
to provide for its needs and to help it to grow. The
departments still using the lab made a natural progression
up the user levels. The moderate users were gradually
becoming heavier users and the occasional users became more
moderate.

177

After two years of operation, we can look back and see the maturation of the Library's microcomputer lab. It is a child with a purpose in life; to develop within the academic environment of its institution and to offer its resources to those who find a need. It is the seed from which other labs are born. It parents the smaller labs which facilitate specific needs for specific groups of people and it opens up new possibilities for those who have not yet experienced its value.

Speakers

RALPH ALBERICO
James Madison University
Reference Department
Carrier Library
Harrisonburg, VA 22807
703/568-6923

BRIAN ALLEY
Sangamon State University
University Library
Springfield, IL 62708
217/786-6597

PAMELA ANDRE
National Agricultural Library
Information Systems Division
Beltsville, MD 20705
301/344-3813

WAYNE ANDREWS
Illinois State University
Provost's Office
Normal, IL 61761
309/438-3481

ELIZABETH S. AVERSA
Catholic University of America
School of Library and
    Information Science
620 Michigan Avenue NE
Washington, DC 20017
202/635-5000

BETH BABIKOW
Baltimore County Public Library
Administrative Services
320 York Road
Towson, MD 21204

C. MARK BATTEY
Addison-Wesley Publishing Company
Information Services
2725 Sand Hill Road
Menlo Park, CA 94025
415/854-0300

JANE BEAUMONT
Consultant
111 Russell Hill
Toronto, Ontario Canada M4V 2S9
416/922-9364

KARL BEISER
Maine Regional Library System
145 Harlow Street
Bangor, ME 04401
207/947-8336

LOIS BELLAMY
The University of Tennessee/Memphis
Health Science Ctr., Stollerman Library
956 Court, Box 14A
Memphis, TN 38163
901/528-6051

JAMES BENSON
St. John's University
Division of Library & Information Science
Grand Central and Utopia Parkway
Jamaica, NY 11439
718/990-6161

REBECCA BILLS
West Virginia College of Graduate Studies
Library
Institute, WV 25112
304/768-9711

RICHARD BAZILLION
Algoma University College
118 Tlain Tress
Sault Ste. Marie, Ontario Canada P6A 2G4
705/949-4352

NEIL BREARLEY
Carleton University Library
Ottawa, Ontario Canada K1S 6J7
613/564-7482

ROBERT W. BURNS, JR.
Colorado State University
Planning and Facilities Management
The Libraries
Fort Collins, CO 80523
303/491-5911

LISA CAMARDO
Raymond Walters College
Computer Support Services
9555 Plainfield Road
Cincinnati, OH 45236
513/745-4318

179

BONNIE CAMPBELL
Ministry of Citizenship and Culture
Libraries & Community Information
  Branch
77 Bloor Street West, 5th Floor
Toronto, Ontario Canada M7A 2R9

ANNE CAPUTO
DIALOG Information Services
Classroom Instruction Program
  Suite 809
1901 North Moore Street
Arlington, VA 22209
703/553-8455

JENNIFER CARGILL
Texas Tech University Libraries
Tech. Processing & Library Automation
  Project
Lubbock, TX 79409-2045
806/742-2261

ROB CARLSON
American Library Association
ALANET
50 East Huron Street
Chicago, IL 60611

JAMES CARROLL
Kansas State Library
State Capitol, 3rd Floor
Topeka, KS 66612-1593
913/296-3296

RICHARD CASSEL
Bureau of State Library/
  Commonwealth of Pennsylvania
Division of School Media Services
333 Market Street
Harrisburg, PA 17108

PHIL CLARK
St. John's University
216 South 4th
Highland Park, NJ 08904

SHARON CLINE
Consultant
6110 Bollinger Road
San Jose, CA 95129

LUCINDA CONGER
U.S. Department of State Library
FAIM/LR, Room 3239 NS
Washington, DC 20520
202/647-8294

JOHN C. COSGRIFF, JR.
Virginia Tech
Newman Library
Blacksburg, VA 24061
703/961-6354

BRUCE COX
Patent Depository Library Program
c/o Ruth Crites
629 Constitution Avenue NE, #204
Washington, DC 20002
202/543-8599

JIM CROOKS
University of Michigan
School of Information &
  Library Science
Ann Arbor, MI 48109

HOWARD CURTIS
Cornell University
Information Technology Section
Mann Library
Ithaca, NY 14853
607/255-2285

PATRICK DEWEY
Maywood Public Library
121 South Fifth Avenue
Maywood, IL 60153

MEL DODD
Texas A&M University
Reference Department
Evans Library
College Station, TX
409/845-8111

REBECCA DUNKLE
The University of Michigan
Systems Office
University Library
Ann Arbor, MI 48109-1185
313/764-0412

180

ELIZABETH EDISON
InMagic, Inc.
2067 Massachusetts Avenue
Cambridge, MA 02140-1138
617/661-8124

DORIS EPLER
Bureau of State Library/
    Commonwealth of Pennsylvania
Division of School Library Media
    Services
333 Market Street
Harrisburg, PA 17108
717/787-6704

MONICA ERTEL
Apple Computer Inc.
Library
20525 Mariani Avenue
Cupertino, CA 95014

DEIRDRE FARRIS
Hillsborough Community College
Ybor City Campus
P.O. Box 75313
Tampa, FL 33675
813/247-6641

LINDY FERNANDEZ
Hillsborough Community College
Ybor City Campus
P.O. Box 75313
Tampa, FL 33675
813/247-6641

DENISE FESMIRE
Methodist Hospitals of Memphis
251 South Claybrook
Memphis, TN 38104-3578
902/726-8862

ERIC FLOWER
University of Maine
Fogler Library
Orono, ME 04469
207/581-1686

GLORIA FULTON
Humboldt State University
Library
Arcata, CA 95521

KELLY GORDON
Central Michigan University
Library, I.P.C.D.
Mt. Pleasant, MI 49959

CHARLENE GRASS
Kansas State University Libraries
Technical Services and Automation
Manhattan, KS 66506
913/532-6516

CLYDE GROTOPHORST
George Mason University
Library
4400 University Drive
Fairfax, VA 22030

JOANNE GUYTON
Methodist Hospitals of Memphis
Education Resources
251 South Claybrook
Memphis, TN 38104-3578
902/726-8862

HAL HALL
Texas A&M University
Stirling Evans Library
College Station, TX 77840

JAMES HAMBLETON
The State Law Library
Supreme Court Building
P.O. Box 12367
Austin, TX 78711-2387
512/463-1722

MAUREEN HARDEN
University of California, San Diego
Library Personnel Office
The University Library
La Jolla, CA 92093
619/534-3063

TONY HARVELL
University of Miami
Richter Library
Coral Gables, FL 33124

J.J. HAYDEN, III
SOLINET
Plaza Level, 400 Colony Square
1201 Peachtree Street NE
Atlanta, GA 30361
404/892-0943

LYNNE MEYERS HAYMAN
Beaver College
Technical Services
Atwood Library
Glenside, PA 19038
215/572-2900

ANNE HESS
California State University
Kennedy Library
5151 State University Drive
Los Angeles, CA 90032
213/224-2265

WILLIAM HOOTON
National Archives
ODISS
Washington, DC 20408
202/523-5524

BONNIE HORNBECK
University of California, San Diego
Library Business Services
The University Library
La Jolla, CA 92093
619/534-1245

STEVE HUNTER
MEDLINK
1440 Main Street
Waltham, MA 02254

GERALDINE HUTCHINS
Texas A&M University
Reference Division
Evans Library
College Station, TX 77843

SHEILA JAEGER
University of Miami
Government Publications
Richter Library
Coral Gables, FL 33124

LEE JAFFE
University of Southern California
Library, Doheny 300
University Park
Los Angeles, CA 90089-0182

DIANE JOHNSON
Infodata Systems Inc.
5205 Leesburg Pike
Falls Church, VA 22041
703/578-3430

ROBERT KERR
The Alexandria Institute
3100 Airport Road
Boulder, CO 80301

DAVE KING
University of Illinois
School of Lib. & Info. Science/
    410 D. K. Hall
1407 W. Gregory Drive
Urbana, IL 61801
217/333-3280

CHRISTINE KISER
George Mason University
Library
4400 University Drive
Fairfax, VA 22030
703/323-2616

NORMAN KLINE
Apple Computer
20525 Mariana Avenue, MS 2TY
Cupertino, CA 95014
408/973-6395

STEPHEN KOSS
Mobius Management Systems, Inc.
One Sheraton Plaza
New Rochelle, NY 10801

LORRI KOSTERICH
Mobius Management Systems, Inc.
One Sheraton Plaza
New Rochelle, NY 10801

NELL S. KREIS
3190 SW 116th Street
David, FL 33330

182

LYNDA KUNTZ
Consultant
8108 Post Oak Road
Potomac, MD 20854
301/340-7428

JAMIE LARUE
Lincoln Library
326 South Seventh
Springfield, IL 62701
217/753-4988

PETER LEPOER
Ohio State University
Health Sciences Library
Columbus, OH 43210
614/422-9810

MICHAEL LODER
Pennsylvania State University
Library, Schuykill Campus
P.O. Box 308, AT 61-South
Schuykill Haven, PA 17972
717/385-4500 x63

FRED LOW
Fiorella LaGuardia Community College
Technical Services, Library
Long Island City, NY 11101

JOHN LOWE
University of California
Division of Library Automation
186 University Hall
Berkeley, CA 94720
415/642-9485

JANE MANDELBAUM
Nat'l Library Service for the Blind
  & Physically Handicapped
Automated Systems Division
Library of Congress
Washington, DC 20540
202/287-9313

NANCY MANDEVILLE
General Foods Technical Center
250 North Street
White Plains, NY 10625
914/335-6827

BILL MANSPEAKER
The University of Michigan
Systems Office
University Library
Ann Arbor, MI 48109
313/764-0412

MARGARET MARTINEZ
9007 Lee Highway
Fairfax, VA 22031

KAREN S. McCONNELL
Gulf States Utilities
Library
P.O. Box 2951
Beaumont, TX 77704
ALANET 1136

DAVID MCDONALD
University of Michigan
Systems Office, 207 UGL
Ann Arbor, MI 48109-1185
313/764-0412

MARY MCMAHON
BRS Information Technologies
Educational Services
555 E. Lancaster Avenue
St. Davids, PA 19087
215/254-0236

SUSAN MILES
Central Michigan University
Library
Mount Pleasant, MI 48859
517/774-3071

R. BRUCE MILLER
Indiana University Libraries
Systems Office
Bloomington, IN 47405
812/335-3403

TODD MILLER
Information Access Corporation
11 Davis Drive
Belmont, CA 94002

183

JOAN MITCHELL
Carnegie Mellon University
Hunt Library
Pittsburgh, PA 15213-3890
412/268-2446

BONNIE MONTJAR
Kennametal, Inc.
Information Systems Devt./
  Tech Info. Center
P.O. Box 231
LaTrobe, PA 15650
412/539-5721

CATHY MOORE
University of Wisconsin/Madison
WILS
464 Memorial Library
Madison, WI 53706

RACHEL MORELAND
Kansas State University
Circulation-Reserves Dept.
Farrell Library
Manhattan, KS 66506
913/532-6516

DOMINICK MORMINO
Library of Congress
Washington, DC 20540
202/287-1678

NANCY MELIN NELSON
42 Grandview Drive
Mt. Kisco, NY 10549
914/666-3394

ALAN NOURIE
Illinois State University
Public Services & Collection
  Development
Milner Library
Normal, IL 61761
309/438-3481

FRANCES OLD
Baltimore County Public Library
Loch Raven Branch
320 York Road
Towson, MD 21204

WILLY OWEN
University of North Carolina
Technical Support
  Administrative Offices
Davis Library 080-A
Chapel Hill, NC 27514
919/962-1301

JUDY PASK
Purdue University
Undergraduate Library
West Lafayette, IN 47907
317/494-6729

ANNETTE PERETZ
Bronx Community College
Sage Learning Center
University Avenue
Bronx, NY 10453

SANDRA PETERSON
Yale University
Government Documents Center
Seeley Mudd Library
New Haven, CT 06511
203/432-3212

BARBARA QUINT
932 11th Street, Apt. 9
Santa Monica, CA 90403
213/394-5535

NORA RAWLINSON
Baltimore County Public Library
Administrative Offices
320 York Road
Towson, MD 21204
301/296-8500

PHILIP ROSE
AT&T Information Systems
Technical Library
11900 North Pecos Street
Denver, CO 80234
303/538-4276

VICTOR ROSENBERG
Personal Bibliographic Software
P.O. Box 4250
Ann Arbor, MI 48106
313/996-1580

ALAN SAMUELS
University of Missouri
School of Library &
  Informational Science
103A Stewart Hall
Columbia, MO 65211
314/882-4044

SCOTT SEAMAN
The Ohio State University
Education Psychology Library
1945 North High Street
Columbus, OH 43201
614/292-6275

SUZANNE SHAW
University of Florida Libraries
Serials Cataloging Section
P.O. Box 12937
Gainesville, FL 32604
904/392-0351

NANCY SIMONET
Dow Jones & Company
P.O. Box 300
Princeton, NJ 08540
609/4522000x2812

SALLY SMALL
The Pennsylvania State University
The Berks Campus Memorial Library
RD #5, Tulpehocken Road
P.O. Box 2150
Reading, PA 19608
215/320-4823

DANA SMITH
Purdue University
Undergraduate Library
West Lafayette, IN 47909
317/494-6729

LYNN SMITH
Indiana University
School of Medicine Library
635 Barnhill Drive
Indianapolis, IN 46223

PAMELA SNELSON
Drew University Library
Madison, NJ 07940

BARNEY STONE
Stone Edge Technologies
P.O. Box 455
Spring House, PA 19477
215/641-1825

NATALIE O. STURR
SUNY Oswego
3 Braniff Drive
Camillus, NY 13031
315/341-4546

JANET SWANBECK
Texas A&M University
Evans Library
College Station, TX 77840
409/845-8111

MARNIE SWANSON
University of Calgary Library
Arts and Humanities Area
2500 University Drive NW
Calgary, Alberta Canada T2N 1N4

ROSEMARY TALAB
Kansas State University
College of Education
Bluemont Hall
Manhattan, KS 66506
913/532-5550

JEANNINE UPPGARD
Westfield State College
Library
Westfield, MA 01086

JANET VRATNY-WATTS
Apple Computer Library
10381 Bandley Drive, 8C
Cupertino, CA 95014

STEVE WATKINS
University of California
University Library
Santa Cruz, CA 95064
408/429-2463

MAGGIE WEAVER
84 Shaftesbury Avenue
Toronto, Ontario Canada M4T 1A5

BECKI WHITAKER
INCOLSA
1100 West 42nd Street
Indianapolis, IN 46208
317/926-3361

FRANK WHITE
Dept. of Finance/Treasury Board of Canada
Library, 11th Floor
L'Esplanade Laurier
Ottawa, Ontario Canada K1A 0G5

BRIAN WILLIAMS
California Poly State University
University Library
San Luis Obispo, CA 93407
805/546-2649

MARK WILSON
Juniata College
Library
Huntingdon, PA 16652
814/643-4310

VIVECA YOSHIKAWA
Hillsborough Community College
Library, Ybor City Campus
P.O. Box 75313
Tampa, FL 33675

Index to Papers by Session and Title

187

188

SESSION SIX: Focus on Design: Systems Analysis, UNIX, and PC-DOS

SESSION SEVEN: Software for Libraries: Part II

SESSION EIGHT: Online Databases and The Tradition of Change: Part II--Online in the Schools

SESSION NINE: Hardware Issues, Part I

190

191

192

Noontime Demonstration

227273